CRAGSMOOR FREE LIBRARY

P.O Box 410 Cragsmoor, NY 12420　　845-647-4611

Library Director　　*Hattie Grifo*

Library Hours

Sunday	*Closed*
Monday	*Closed*
Tuesday	*9:30am–6:00pm*
Wednesday	*Closed*
Thursday	*11:00am–7:30pm*
Friday	*3:30pm–5:00pm*
Saturday	*9:30am–4:30pm*

LIBRARY HISTORY

The hamlet of Cragsmoor, an area of approximately one square mile, is located near Ellenville, NY on State Route 52 between Ellenville and Pine Bush. Cragsmoor, originally founded as a farming community in the early 1800's, became an art colony at the turn of the century. Most of the artist's homes still survive and constitute the area that is a National Historic District.

The Library was started by the artists, their spouses and many local residents who obtained a provisional Charter from New York State in 1913. The books were donated and kept in several locations until Frederick S. Dellenbaugh (explorer, author and artist) donated the land and designed the Library building.

It was built in 1923 by local craftsmen (some of those families still live here), and opened to the public in 1925. The Cragsmoor Free Library received its permanent charter in 1949 as an Association Library and has been in service to the public ever since.

The founders of the Cragsmoor Art Colony and their contemporaries have donated many works to the library. These gifts have created a unique collection which is augmented by our present day artists. More artists live and work here today than during the time of the original art colony.

The Library is a community center. In addition to books, books on tape, DVDs, newspapers and magazines, there are several computers, WiFi capability, and many programs are offered during the year, educational and fun, to appeal to both children and adults. Because the library not a town or school library, less than half of it's annual operating budget comes from public funding. The rest must be privately raised.

In the 1980's the Library received a grant to pursue the admittance of Cragsmoor to the National Register. On August 7, 1996 the Cragsmoor Historic District became part of the National Register of Historic Places.

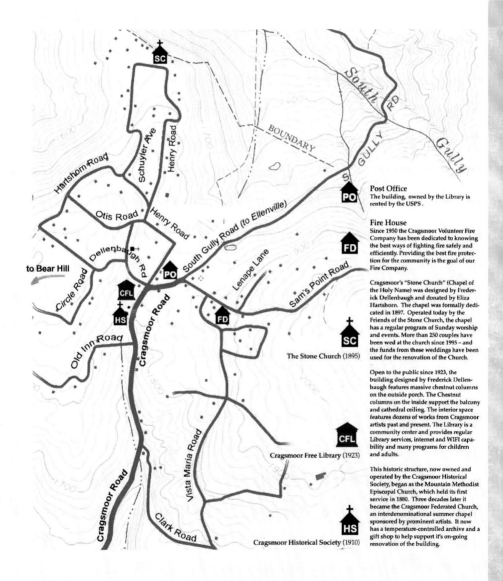

Post Office
The building, owned by the Library is rented by the USPS .

Fire House
Since 1950 the Cragsmoor Volunteer Fire Company has been dedicated to knowing the best ways of fighting fire safely and efficiently. Providing the best fire protection for the community is the goal of our Fire Company.

Cragsmoor's "Stone Church" (Chapel of the Holy Name) was designed by Frederick Dellenbaugh and donated by Eliza Hartshorn. The chapel was formally dedicated in 1897. Operated today by the Friends of the Stone Church, the chapel has a regular program of Sunday worship and events. More than 250 couples have been wed at the church since 1995 – and the funds from these weddings have been used for the renovation of the Church.

Open to the public since 1923, the building designed by Frederick Dellenbaugh features massive chestnut columns on the outside porch. The Chestnut columns on the inside support the balcony and cathedral ceiling. The interior space features dozens of works from Cragsmoor artists past and present. The Library is a community center and provides regular Library services, internet and WIFI capability and many programs for children and adults.

This historic structure, now owned and operated by the Cragsmoor Historical Society, began as the Mountain Methodist Episcopal Church, which held its first service in 1880. Three decades later it became the Cragsmoor Federated Church, an interdenominational summer chapel sponsored by prominent artists. It now has a temperature-controlled archive and a gift shop to help support it's on-going renovation of the building.

The Stone Church (1895)

Cragsmoor Free Library (1923)

Cragsmoor Historical Society (1910)

ACKNOWLEDGEMENTS

The Cragsmoor Free Library would like to thank everyone who took the time to contribute recipes for this cookbook. Without your generous submissions, this project would not have been possible.

Thank you also to those who contributed their time and talents to create this cookbook:

• **Rebekah Leonard** for coordinating the project and bringing it to fruition, balancing just the right ingredients of humor and relentless determination.

• **John Duncan** for doing the layout of all our dividers, information page and map, as well as creating the front and back covers using beautiful photographs taken by:
  Pat Peters (front cover picture of the Cragsmoor Library)
  Hattie Grifo (back cover picture of Bear Hill)

• **Mary Ann Maurer** for her tireless efforts in handling all the little last-minute details, as well as cajoling recipes from Cragsmoor residents near and far.

• **John Hart** for doing the black and white sketch of the Library.

Austa Densmore Sturdevant (1855-1936) was primarily a portrait painter. She joined the Art Student's League in New York City and studied under Raphael Collin in Paris. Her work hangs in the New York State Museum, The National Portrait Gallery and many private collections, galleries and museums. Her paintings in this cookbook appear courtesy of the Cragsmoor Free Library.

TABLE OF CONTENTS

 In Loving Memory

These recipes have been typed and proofed by:

Rebekah Leonard, Typist
Mary Ann Maurer, Typist
Rebekah Leonard, Proofreader

Printed in the U.S.A. by
Fundcraft Publishing
P.O. Box 340 Collierville, TN 38027
800.853.1363   www.fundcraft.com

Poppies
Austa Densmore Sturdevant (1855-1936)

Recipe Favorites

Page No.

Recipe Title:_____

_____   _____

_____   _____

_____   _____

_____   _____

_____   _____

_____   _____

_____   _____

_____   _____

_____   _____

_____   _____

Page No.

Family Favorites

Recipe Title:_____

_____   _____

_____   _____

_____   _____

_____   _____

_____   _____

Notes:_____

_____

_____

_____

702-08

APPETIZERS

ANTI-PASTA

1-14 oz can artichoke hearts, drained
1-14 oz can pitted lg. Ripe olives, drained
½ c sliced green onion-tops included
1-6.5 oz jar Italian style roasted sweet red peppers, drained

1 lb cheese (cheddar, Monterrey jack, Munster or swiss
1 clove garlic minced
¾ tsp. Dried crushed oregano or basil leaves
⅓ cup olive oil
½ cup red wine vinegar
Salt to taste
½ tsp black pepper

Cut artichokes into quarters. Put into 1.5 qt. Container w/tight fitting cover. Add olives & onions. Cut peppers into 1" squares & cut cheese into ½" cubes.

Combine garlic, oregano or basil, olive oil, vinegar, salt, & pepper in small jar. Shake until blended. Pour over ingredients. Cover bowl & shake gently 1 min. Refrigerate at least 3 hrs. - shaking once each hour. Drain & reserve marinade & ingredients. Leave @ room temperature for 1 hr. Transfer to serving dish. Place marinade in small bowl to serve with vegetables.

Theresa Capobianco

Tip-Marinate each ingredient separately & arrange in mounds on serving dish

ARTICHOKE DIP

2 cans artichoke hearts drained and chopped
1 jar (8 oz.) Parmesan cheese

1 jar (15 oz.) Hellmann's Reduced mayonnaise

Mix all ingredients together and bake in a shallow dish at 300°F for about 20 minutes and serve.

Deena Davidson

SPINACH ARTICHOKE DIP

1 cup mayonnaise
1 cup parmesan cheese
2 cloves garlic, minced

1 package chopped frozen
spinach
1 14½ oz. can artichoke
hearts, chopped

Preheat oven to 350°F. Thaw and drain spinach. Combine all ingredients in a casserole and mix thoroughly. Place in the oven and bake until bubbly, approximately 30-35 minutes. Serve with a variety of crackers or in a bread bowl with bread chunks for dipping.

Rebekah Leonard

DOC'S HOT CLAM DIP

2 6 ½ oz. cans minced clams
2 tsp lemon juice
½ cup seasoned bread
crumbs
1 stick butter
1 small onion, grated
½ green pepper, grated

1 clove garlic, minced
1 tsp oregano
1 tsp parsley
dash Tabasco
Romano cheese
Paprika

In saucepan, place minced clams with juice; add lemon juice. Simmer 4 minutes. In frying pan, melt butter, add onion, pepper, garlic, oregano, parsley and Tabasco. Saute 5 minutes. Add clams to frying pan mixture along with ½ cup seasoned bread crumbs. Pour mixture into baking dish. Sprinkle with grated Romano cheese and paprika. Bake at 400°F until bubbly. Serve with crackers.

Dr. Ben Colucci

* * * * *

I do not like broccoli. And I haven't liked it since I was a little kid and my mother made me eat it. And I'm President of the United States and I'm not going to eat any more broccoli.

George Bush, U.S. President

HOT CRAB DIP

1 lb crab meat - claw or
  special
1 lg cream cheese - softened
8 oz sour cream
4 tbs. mayo

1 ½ tbs lemon juice
1 tbs dry mustard
⅛ tsp garlic salt
½ c + ¼ c grated cheddar
  cheese

Mix together except ¼ c grated cheese. Put in oven proof baking dish sprinkle with ¼ c cheese and bake at 325°F for 30 minutes or until it bubbles.

Wanda Cooke

Serve hot with bread cubes, firm crackers or carrot sticks.

MICHELLE'S HUMMUS

1 can chick peas, mostly
  drained
1 clove garlic

¼ c. tahini
¼ c. lemon juice
pince of salt

Combine in food processor.

David McAlpin

* * * * *

A loaf of bread, the Walrus said,
Is what we chiefly need:
Pepper and vinegar besides
Are very good indeed
Now if you're ready, Oysters, dear,
We can begin to feed!
Lewis Carroll
(Alice Through the Looking-Glass)

HUMUS FROM AN INDIFFERENT COOK

2 c raw chickpeas
5 cloves or more garlic
1 ½ tsp salt
¼ to ⅓ c lemon juice or 1 c
  tahini

¼ to ⅓ c apple cider vinegar
  or ¼ c olive oil
1 Tbs. black pepper
(¼ to ½ cup of water or
  cooking liquid if needed
  for smooth consistency)

Possible additions depending on your taste: ½ cup sauteed red or yellow pepper or marinated artichoke hearts, or ¼ cup sauteed garlic.

Possible seasonings: ¼ cup fresh parsley, 2 Tbs dry thyme, hot pepper sauce, tamari.

1. Soak chick peas in water (about 2 inches above the chickpeas) the night before. Cover and refrigerate.
2. Cook chickpeas till soft (approximately 1 hr). Then drain. (I save some of the liquid to use for thinning if needed.)
3. Place all measured liquids in a large Pyrex measuring cup or other vessel with a spout.
4. Using a food processor or food mill, combine chickpeas, garlic and tahini while slowly adding the liquids to consistency desired. (The slow addition keeps the processor from jamming.)
5. Add any additional seasonings or other additions from above. Run through food mill or processor until smooth, creamy consistency.
6. Chill thoroughly.

Joan Lesikin

High in protein, humus, is a great meat substitute. As a meal, serve on pita or heavy bread with a garden salad. Stores well in fridge for several days. Freezing changes texture.

* * * * *

Every hard boiled egg has a soft center.
Mark Twain

SUNFLOWER SPREAD

1 7 oz jar sunflower nuts
3 5 oz jars Old English
cheese

1 12 oz pkg. softened cream
cheese
1 tsp garlic
1 tbs parsley

Put nuts in a food processor & chop. Add everything else & process till blended. Refrigerate, then serve it at room temperature.

Dee Sherry

OLIVE TAPENADE
(A party favorite.)

6 anchovies preserved in salt
(or 2 Tbsp anchovy paste
from a tube)
13 oz. black olives in brine,
pitted (or nicoise olive
paste from a jar)
1 small clove garlic, coarsely
chopped

3 Tbsp capers, rinsed and
drained
2 tsp strong mustard
2 Tbsp Cognac
$2/3$ extra virgin olive oil
fresh ground pepper

For serving: country or rye bread.
Rinse anchovies under cold running water and rub them to remove all traces of salt. Separate into fillets, removing the head and backbone. Cut each fillet into small pieces. Combine anchovies, olives, garlic and capers in a food processor. Add mustard, Cognac, pepper and half the oil and blend to a thick paste; while continuing to blend pour in the rest of the oil. When the tapenade is smooth, transfer to a serving bowl. Serve with slices of bread, plain or toasted. Tapenade may be kept refrigerated for several weeks in a sealed container. Bring to room temperature before using. Makes 25-30 servings.

John Duncan

SPINACH BITES

2 pkgs. frozen chopped
  spinach, thawed and
  drained
2 cups Pepperidge Farms
  stuffing
1 onion, chopped

4 eggs, beaten (or used Egg
  Beaters)
½ cup melted butter or
  margarine
½ cup grated Parmesan
  cheese

Preheat oven to 375°F. Combine all ingredients in a large bowl. Form into bite-sized balls and place on lightly buttered (or sprayed with Pam) cookie sheet. Bake for 20 minutes. Serve alone or with a dip. (Ranch or Sweet and Sour sauce) Yields 36 spinach balls.

Note: Spinach balls can be frozen on a cookie sheet and then placed in freezer bags for future use. Defrost 20 minutes before baking and then bake as above.

Bev Simonelli

ZUCCHINI APPETIZER

3 c thinly sliced zucchini
1 c Bisquick Baking mix
½ c finely chopped onion
2 tbs fresh parsley
½ c grated parmesan cheese
½ tsp salt

½ tsp dried marjoram or
  oregano
dash of pepper
1 clove of garlic finely
  chopped
½ c vegetable oil
4 eggs slightly beaten

Heat oven to 350°F. Grease a 9x13x2 inch pan. Mix all ingredients together well. Pour into pan and bake until golden brown - about 25 minutes. Cool slightly and cut into 2x1 inch pieces. Serve warm.

Betty Tamburo

* * * * *

Chicken salad has a certain glamour about it! Like the little black dress, it is chic and adaptable and can be taken anywhere.

Laurie Colwin

CHILLED ASPARAGUS

8 or more thin asparagus (at least 2 per person)
softened cream cheese
1 clove garlic finely chopped

chopped fresh dill (dried dill can be substituted)
Deli salmon, thinly sliced

Barely cook asparagus - should still be crisp. Let cool. Mix softened cream cheese with garlic and dill to taste. Roll a piece of salmon around the middle of the asparagus spear and seal it together with the cream cheese mixture. Refrigerate until ready to use. Arrange on a platter, decorate with lettuce and cherry tomatoes.

Mary Ann Maurer

STUFFED MUSHROOMS

3 lbs. (stuffing) mushrooms
1 & ½ sticks of butter
1 & ½ cups bread crumbs (Italian style)
6 cloves garlic

salt
3 Tbsp grated parmesan cheese
water if needed

Wash and dry mushrooms. Remove stems from caps and chop coarsely (a mini-chopper works well). Saute stems in melted butter for a few minutes. Crush garlic in a press and add to the frying pan for a few more minutes. Stir in bread crumbs and saute briefly. If the mix is too stiff add a bit of water. Let cool briefly. Stir in salt (to taste) and cheese. Put caps on a buttered cookie sheet. Bake at 400°F for 10-15 minutes or until sides of caps begin to fall and pull away from stuffing.

Jack Grifo

Can be made the day ahead and baked, or reheated when ready to serve.

* * * * *

When life gives you lemons, make lemonade.

BACON AND TOMATO CANAPE

Rounds of bread
sliced bacon
large red tomatoes - sliced

cucumber - sliced
stuffed olives - sliced
Mayonnaise

Make consistent bread rounds by using a glass to cut the bread, then toast the rounds. Cook the bacon until crisp, mix it with mayonnaise. Spread the bacon, mayo mixture on the toasted bread. Add a slice of tomato, then a slice of cucumber and garnish with a slice of stuffed olive and serve.

Wyona Maurer

The amounts are determined by the number of guests. As a guide, 1 large tomato would make 8 to 10 slices. Leftover bacon mixture can be used for sandwiches at another time.

PICKLED SHRIMP

1 large lemon
1 ½ tsp coriander seeds
3 Tbsp white wine vinegar
1 Tbsp olive oil
1 Tbsp water
1 Tbsp sugar
¼ tsp dried hot pepper
  flakes

1 Tbsp plus 2 ½ tsp Kosher
  salt
2 Tbsp pickling spices
1 lb large shrimp, shelled
  and deveined (No need to
  thaw shrimp if frozen. Just
  throw them into the
  boiling water and cook a
  little longer until done)

Remove zest from lemon with a zester (or with a vegetable peeler) and remove with pith from zest strips with sharp knife. Juice the lemon and finely grind the coriander seeds. Whisk together in a large bowl with the vinegar, oil, water, sugar, hot pepper flakes and 2 ½ tsp of salt until sugar and salt are dissolved. Meanwhile, bring a 3-4 qt pot of water to boil with pickling spices and remaining 1 Tbsp of salt and cook shrimp 1 ½ minutes or until just cooked through. Transfer shrimp with a slotted spoon to marinade, tossing to coat. Cool shrimp slightly and transfer shrimp and marinade to a large, sealed plastic bag. Marinate, chilled, turning bag occasionally, at least 8 hours. Drain shrimp before serving.

John Duncan

RED PEPPER SHRIMP TOASTS

2 garlic cloves
¼ tsp cayenne pepper
⅛ tsp crumbled saffron
   threads
½ cup diced, drained roasted
   red pepper from jar, patted
   dry

2 tsp red wine vinegar
½ cup mayonnaise
24 uncooked large shrimp,
   peeled, deveined
12 4x½ inch diagonal slices
   sourdough baguette
¼ cup drained capers

Rouille: Finely chop garlic cloves with cayenne pepper and saffron in mini food processor. Add roasted pepper and vinegar to processor; blend until smooth. Blend in mayonnaise. Season to taste with salt and pepper. Can be made in advance and refrigerated.

Shrimp Toasts: Preheat oven to 425°F. Transfer ⅓ cup rouille to medium bowl with shrimp. Toss to coat. Arrange bread slices on baking sheet. Spread each slice with rouille. Bake until toast bottoms are crisp and rouille is darker in color, about 10 minutes. Heat large, non-stick skillet over medium-high heat. Add shrimp in a single layer. Cook until just browned and opaque in center, about 2 minutes on each side. Arrange toasts on plate and place shrimp on each toast; sprinkle toasts with capers. Makes 12.

John Duncan

SHRIMP DELIGHT

1 c mayonnaise
½ c sour cream
1 tbs fresh parsley, chopped
3 cans small shrimp, drained

1 tbs sherry
1 tsp lemon juice
salt & pepper to taste

Mix all ingredients together and refrigerate at least one hour before serving. Serve with crackers, crusty bread or vegetable sticks

Estella Greenawalt

STUFFED VEAL CUTLETS

1 lb veal cutlets
¼ lb ham
1 egg

1 cup seasoned bread
  crumbs
garlic powder
grated parmesan cheese

Cut veal cutlets into small squares (approximately 1 ½ inches). Top with a piece of ham. Sprinkle garlic powder, cheese and pepper (No salt). Roll and pin with a toothpick (the round kind). Dip in slightly beaten egg and roll in seasoned bread crumbs. Fry in olive oil slowly (may be deep fried also). Serve on platter with black olives, roasted peppers and celery. Serves 2 to 4. Delicious.

Lois Colucci

SAUSAGE BREAD

Frozen Pizza dough
Parmesan Cheese
Several links of sausage

½ can of mushrooms,
  drained
Mozzarella Cheese

Thaw the dough, take the sausage out of the casing and fully cook (fry) Grate the mozzarella cheese. Flour the surface to be used for rolling the dough, and roll the dough out careful not to roll it too thin. Fill the center with the cooled, drained sausage meat, top with drained mushrooms and cover first with parmesan cheese, then grated mozzarella. Mozzarella is the secret! So be generous. Fold the sides over the meat like a trifold. Bake at 350°F for 20 minutes or until golden brown.

Jeane Noud

Let cool before you cut it.

* * * * *

Coffee, chocolate, men...
Some things are just better when they are rich.

SOUPS & SALADS

White Bearded Iris
Austa Densmore Sturdevant (1855-1936)

Recipe Favorites

Page No.

Recipe Title:_____   _____

_____   _____

_____   _____

_____   _____

_____   _____

_____   _____

_____   _____

_____   _____

_____   _____

_____   _____

Family Favorites

Page No.

Recipe Title:_____   _____

_____   _____

_____   _____

_____   _____

_____   _____

Notes:_____

_____

_____

_____

702-08

SOUPS & SALADS

HEARTY VEGETABLE SOUP

4 large potatoes, peeled and
  cubed
4 large carrots, peeled and
  sliced
2 large parsnips, peeled and
  sliced
1 cup petite frozen peas
1 large yellow onion,
  chopped

1 large leek (white part only)
  well washed, chopped
3 Tbsp olive oil
1 bay leaf
2 cubes Knorr vegetable
  broth
salt and pepper

Saute chopped onions and the leek until lightly browned, add potatoes, carrots, parsnips and bay leaf, add water until all veggies are just covered. Bring to a boil, then simmer on low heat until all veggies are soft, about 25 minutes. Add frozen peas and broth cubes and let simmer for another 5 minutes. Add salt and pepper to taste. If you like soup less chunky you can mash the veggies n the pot with a potato masher or put some of it in a blender and re-add to the soup. This is your basic great winter veggie soup and goes well with any bread and cheese lunch. Reheats well after refrigerator storage or frozen in baggies. Serves 4-6.

Irene Seeland

EGYPTIAN LENTIL SOUP

1 cup orange lentils
1 large onion, chopped
2 carrots, sliced
3 tsp cumin
1 tsp ground cardamom

1 Tbsp butter or margarine
4 cups water
2 tomatoes sliced
1 tsp salt
2 chicken bouillon cubes

Rinse lentils and drain. Saute onion with butter in saucepan. Add all other ingredients. Cover and simmer for one hour. Puree in blender. Adjust seasoning if desired. Serves 5-6. Sprinkle toasted croutons on top.

Mary Davidson

ZUCCHINI STEW

¼ cup olive oil
6 cloves garlic, chopped fine
3 large zucchini (the ones that get really big from the garden but are still tender, if you can pierce the skin with a fingernail, they are fine, if seeds are big take them out)
1 russet potato, chopped into one inch cubes with skin on
2-3 tomatoes, chopped
salt & pepper to taste

Heat oil in large pan. Add garlic and saute until translucent, do not brown. Add zucchini and potato and saute until soft and stew-like. Add tomatoes near the end and then add salt and pepper to taste. Serve with lots of fresh grated Parmesan cheese. Serves 6

Angelena Abate, from my Grandmother

LENTIL EGGPLANT STEW

2 c lentils
2 qt vegetable stock or water
1 medium onion, chopped
¾ c olive oil
1 medium eggplant
1 can (6 oz) tomato paste
2 c celery, chopped
1 t oregano
1 t basil
3 gloves garlic, mashed
salt & pepper to taste
¼ wine vinegar

Put water or stock and lentils into soup pot and bring to a boil. Simmer 1 ½ hours. Saute onion and celery in olive oil til soft. Transfer into pot with a slotted spoon. Cut eggplant into ½ in. cubes and soften in remaining oil (may need extra). Add to pot with remaining ingredients. Simmer 1 hr or until lentils are tender. Add water if necessary. Serves 5-6.

Jack Grifo

If you find yourself without celery and or tomato paste, you can substitute celery seeds or 2 fresh tomatoes. Wine vinegar can be increased to about 1/3 cup.

DELICIOUS PASTA SOUP

1 Tbsp olive oil
2 minced garlic cloves
26 oz. Cragsmoor water
2 vegetable bouillon cubes
½ cup elbow pasta

1 15.5 oz can chickpeas,
  drained and rinsed
2 Tbsp fresh parsley,
  chopped
ground black pepper
grated parmesan

Saute garlic in the olive oil 1-2 minutes. Add water and bouillon cubes and bring to a boil. Add pasta and chickpeas. Cook about 5 minutes, or until pasta is al dente. Serve with parsley and sprinkle with pepper and parmesan cheese.

Tom Bolger

SPINACH RAVIOLI SOUP

4 cups chicken broth
5-6 oz. fresh spinach
9 oz. frozen cheese ravioli
  (small)

1 egg, beaten
parmesan cheese

Cook broth, spinach and ravioli until ravioli is done. Add beaten egg. Serve with parmesan cheese. Enjoy.

Anonymous

MINESTRONE WITH TORTELLINI

1 large onion, cut in a large
  dice
4 large carrots, peeled and
  sliced
1 fennel bulb, sliced
2 large potatoes, cut in large
  dice
1 green pepper
2 Zucchini, cut in large dice

1 ½ cup green beans 1 inch
  pieces
2 cups cabbage shredded
10 cups chicken stock
1 28 oz. chopped tomatoes
2 T. oregano
2 T. basil
1 lb. cheese tortellini

Put all of the ingredients except the tortellini in to a large stock pot and bring to a boil. Reduce the heat and simmer for 2 to 3 hours stirring occasionally. Cook the tortellini separately and add to soup 5 minutes before serving. Garnish the soup with a heaping tablespoon of grated Parmesan cheese.

Lee Ann Leichtfuss

TOMATO-TORTELLINI SOUP

2 14 oz cans of chicken broth
1 9 oz pkg refrigerated
  tortellini, prepared
  according to pkg
  directions

½ 8 oz tub onion and chives
  cream cheese
1 11 oz can condensed
  tomato bisque soup
snipped chives

In a bowl, whisk ⅓ cup hot broth into cream cheese until smooth and put it in a saucepan. Add all ingredients except chives and heat through. Sprinkle with chives before serving.

Anonymous

This recipe is beyond simple. It can be doubled or more.

* * * * *

The breakfast food idea made its appearance in a little third-story room on the corner of 28th Street and Third Avenue, New York City....My cooking facilities were very limited, [making it] very difficult to prepare cereals. It often occurred to me that it should be possible to purchase cereals at groceries already cooked and ready to eat, and I considered different ways in which this might be done.

John Harvey Kellogg

WICKED GOOD GARBANZO TOMATO SOUP

Garbanzo beans (2 large cans)
Crushed tomatoes (1 large can) preferably with Basil. If you can't find cans with basil then make sure to add fresh basil.
1 red or green pepper (large)

1 medium sized onion
three large carrots or equivalent baby carrots
at least half a container of cut up mushrooms not more than a container
about half a bag of frozen corn

(If you have some other favorite vegetable go ahead and add it!)

All the herbs and spices are to taste but don't add more than a teaspoon to start with the first time you make it.

salt and pepper
ginger powder
curry powder
oregano

and anything else you think would taste good
olive oil and a large sauce pan.

Finely chop the Garlic.

Cut the onions and peppers into half inch squares and cut the carrots into quarter inch slices and then cut the wide bits in half so that they cook evenly.

Use enough oil to cover the bottom of the pan and the garlic. when the garlic is starting to brown add the curry powder. before the curry burns add the peppers, onions and carrots. Make sure they cover the pan and then let them sit for a little bit to absorb the curry. Then stir them occasionally until well cooked.

Add the garbanzo beans after you have drained most of the liquid from the cans. Stir those in and let simmer for about five min or so and stir occasionally. During that time add the other herbs and spices. Once that smells good and feels kind of soft add the tomatoes and stir those in. Then add the corn. Allow this to all simmer on a medium-low heat for about 15-20 min. and stir occasionally. You don't want any of it to stick to the bottom of the pot.

If you would like to make it smoother and creamier you can blend a portion of it in the blender. I would wait until it cools before doing so. Serve with a dollop of sour cream or lactaid free cottage cheese for an extra punch

Jenn MacGregor

CREAMY CAULIFLOWER SOUP WITH CHORIZO AND GREENS

(Used by Permission from "Sara's Secrets for Weeknight Meals", Broadway Books, 2005.)

This is a very substantial and satisfying soup. thickened by pureed cauliflower and potato, it is luxuriously creamy without any cream. The sausage, greens, and paprika give it heat, and the cauliflower florets give it crunch. Serve this soup with a nice green salad and you've got a meal in a bowl.

2 tablespoons extra virgin olive oil
10 ounces chorizo or andouille sausage, sliced
1 medium onion, sliced (about 1 cup)
1 medium head cauliflower (about 2 pounds)
1 small Yukon gold potato (about 4 ounces)
4 cups chicken broth

1 bunch mustard greens, kale, or spinach, or a mixture, rinsed, dried, and sliced
3 tablespoons fresh lemon juice
Kosher salt and freshly milled black pepper
Paprika, preferably smoked for garnish
Grilled or broiled slices of homemade-style bread, rubbed with a cut garlic clove, optional

Heat the oil in a large saucepan over high heat until hot. Reduce the heat to medium, add the chorizo, and cook, stirring occasionally, until the pieces are lightly browned on both sides, about 5 minutes. Transfer the chorizo with a slotted spoon to a plate. Add the onion to the pan and cook, stirring occasionally, until softened, about 5 minutes.

Meanwhile, cut 2 cups of small florets from the cauliflower and chop the rest. Peel and thinly slice the potato. When the onion has softened, add the chicken broth, chopped cauliflower, and potato to the saucepan; bring the mixture to a boil over high heat. Reduce the heat to low and simmer for about 8 minutes or until the cauliflower and potato are very tender. Transfer to a blender in three or four small batches and puree until very smooth.

Measure the pureed soup and return it to the saucepan. Add water, if necessary, to make 7 cups. Stir in the cauliflower flowerets and simmer for 4 minutes or until they are almost tender. If you are using mustard greens or kale, add them to the soup with the florets. When the florets are just tender, stir in the chorizo and lemon juice; add salt and pepper to taste. If using spinach, stir it in with the chorizo. Ladle the soup into bowls; sprinkle each with some paprika and serve with garlic bread, if desired.

Sara Moulton

Sara Moulton is host of the PBS show, "Sara's Weeknight Meals", executive chef Gourmet Magazine and food editor, Good Morning America.

HAM AND CHEESE SOUP

2 cups diced potatoes
8 oz shredded cheese
1 cup ham, cubed
½ cup diced carrots

½ cup sliced celery
¼ cup chopped onion
1 ½ tsp salt
¼ tsp pepper

Combine ingredients in a saucepan, add 2 cups boiling water. Cook until tender. Meanwhile make a white sauce as follows: ¼ cup oleo, ¼ cup flour, 2 cups milk and add 8 oz. shredded cheese. Heat until melted stirring often. Add one cup cubed ham and undrained veggies. May need a little more salt and pepper.

Chris Stedner

* * * * *

O, blackberry tart, with berries as big as your thumb, purple and black, and thick with juice, and a crust to endear them that will go to cream in your mouth, and both passing down with such a taste that will make you close your eyes and wish you might live forever in the wideness of that rich moment.

Richard Llewellyn, Welsh Novelist

MARYLAND CRAB SOUP

1 lb crab meat (regular or
  claw)
1 chicken bouillon cube
1 c boiling water
¼ c chopped onion
¼ c butter
2 tbs flour
1 tsp salt

¼ tsp celery salt
¼ tsp pepper
1 quart milk
½ c sherry
a few drops of hot sauce (to
  taste)
parsley for garnish

Dissolve the bouillon in water. In a 4 quart saucepan cook the onion in butter till translucent. Blend in the flour. Add all seasonings. Gradually add the milk to the mixture and cook over medium heat until it is thick enough to coat a spoon. Add crab meat and sherry. Cook until they are thoroughly integrated, do not allow the soup to boil. Serve at once or refrigerate. If you refrigerate the soup, let it come to room temperature before slowly re-heating it.

Inez Ferrar

SCALLOP, CRAB &FISH CHOWDER

¾ c sliced sweet onions
½ c dry white wine
3 c fish stock*
1 c water
1 lb small red potatoes
  peeled and halved
Salt and freshly ground
  white pepper
½ c heavy cream

1 tbs olive oil
2 tbs butter
4 oz crabmeat
6-8 oz firm white fish
  (flounder, perch etc)
6 large sea scallops, halved
1 tbs chopped fresh dill
Lemon zest to taste

Sauté onions until caramelized. Deglaze the pot with white wine, get all the browned bits in the bottom of the pot.

Add the potatoes, stock and water and season with salt and pepper. Raise the heat and boil gently until the potatoes are tender, 10 to 15 minutes. Add the cream to the stock and simmer. Remove from the heat until ready to serve.

Cook crab, scallops and fish in a frying pan with 2 tablespoons of butter until just done. Reheat the soup. Add the dill and lemon zest and stir. Taste to adjust the seasoning. Divide the warmed crab, scallops and fish among warmed bowls. Ladle the soup over and serve immediately.

Mary Ann Maurer

GAZPACHO

6 tomatoes
2 red sweet peppers
2 onions (or less)
2 shallots (or less)
2 cucumbers
2 cups canned tomato juice

½ cup red wine vinegar
½ cup olive oil
½ cup fresh chopped dill
cayenne pepper
salt and pepper

Chop tomatoes, peppers, onions and cucumbers. Mix together. Puree ⅓ of mixture in a blender. Add oil, vinegar, dill, spices and tomato juice. Serve cold topped with croutons.

Elfi Roze-Avinger

3 FAST & EASY SOUP VARIATIONS

Brown fresh or canned mushrooms in butter, add a can of mushroom soup mixed with light cream and sherry. The addition of chopped boiled egg makes this a really hearty soup.

NOTE: a touch of sherry takes the "canned" taste away.

To a can of tomato bisque, add canned tomatoes, juice and all, a drop or two of hot sauce, cream or sour cream to taste. Heat, and top with thinly sliced scallions. Start with a can of cream of celery soup, add milk or cream, a little freshly grated nutmeg and thin slices of apple.

Dianne Wiebe

JICAMA SALAD

1 lb Jicama, peeled
½ cup thinly sliced red
  onion
¼ cup orange juice
2 Tbsp lime juice
1 Tbsp distilled white
  vinegar

2 tsp olive or vegetable oil
2 Tbsp minced parsley
2 Tbsp NutraSweet Spoonful
1 Tbsp finely chopped
  shallot or onion
1 Tbsp grated orange rind
⅛ tsp pepper

Cut Jicama into thick julienne strips. Combine jicama and red onion in serving bowl. Combine remaining ingredients in a covered jar; shake to mix. Pour dressing over jicama and toss. Easy, simple, and delicious

Thomas Bolger

GERMAN COLD SLAW

1 c sour cream
3 tbs sugar
¼ c vinegar

3 c finely shredded cabbage
salt & pepper

Mix sour cream, sugar, salt and pepper. Stir in vinegar slowly. Thoroughly mix with the cabbage. Chill before serving. Serves 6.

Wyona Baeke Maurer

CELERY SALAD

2 lbs. celeriac (knob celery)
1 onion
vinegar
salt to taste

freshly ground pepper to
taste
sugar to taste

1. Scrub celery knobs with stiff brush. Boil in salt water till soft. Remove from liquid and let celery knobs cool. Reserve liquid.
2. When celery knobs are cool, peel them and slice them vertically from the root end up.
3. Mince onion.
4. Make strong vinaigrette using salt, pepper, sugar, vinegar and some of liquid used to boil the celery knobs. Stir in celery knob slices (vinaigrette should cover them) and chill overnight in refrigerator.

Leni Kroul

GERMAN RED BEET SALAD

6 medium red beets, boiled
(45 minutes), peeled and
cubed
2 tart apples, peeled, cored,
cubed

3 large sweet sour pickles,
cubed
3 Tbsp olive oil
2 tsp lemon juice
salt and pepper

Mix the above ingredients with olive oil and lemon juice, add salt and pepper to taste. This is a tasty and fairly low calorie salad that goes nicely with a good brie sandwich. It can also be done with some mayonnaise instead of the olive oil and lemon juice.

Irene Seeland

COLD PEA SALAD

1 20 oz. pkg frozen peas
1 cup chopped celery
1 small onion, chopped
¾ cup mayonnaise

1 Tbsp lemon juice
1 tsp soy sauce
⅛ tsp curry powder
⅛ tsp garlic salt

Defrost but don't cook peas. Mix with celery and onions. Make a dressing by combining next five ingredients and chill. When ready to serve toss pea mixture with dressing. Serves 12. You can also add crab meat, shrimp or tuna.

Bev Simonelli

AVOCADO CORN SALAD.

Start by mixing in a big bowl the following:

⅓ c red wine vinegar,
¼ c fresh lime juice,
2 T olive oil,
2 t cumin,
½ to 1 t red pepper flakes,

½ to 1 t oregano or Italian
   seasoning,
salt and pepper
2-4 cloves of garlic, very
   finely chopped.

To this, add:

2 c lightly steamed corn,

cubed avocados, 2 large or 3
   small.

Mix carefully so you don't squash the avocado, but make sure you coat it with the oil and vinegar so that it doesn't turn brown. Make at least 4 hours ahead, serve chilled or at room temperature.

Dianne Wiebe

* * * * *

I always eat my peas with honey;
I've done it all my life.
They do taste kind of funny but
It keeps them on my knife.
Anonymous

GERMAN POTATO SALAD

3 lbs potatoes	2 tbs chopped parsley
½ c onions chopped	8 slices of bacon
½ c celery chopped	1 well beaten egg yolk

Dressing:

1 tbs flour	1 tsp sugar
⅓ c vinegar	salt & pepper to taste
⅔ c water	

Fry bacon until crisp.

Cut potatoes to bite sized pieces and cook until almost done - potatoes should be firm not mushy Drain potatoes and in large bowl add potatoes, onion, celery, parsley, and bacon

Boil dressing ingredients until slightly thickened and pour over potato mixture. Add beaten egg and mix well. Serve warm.

Anastasia Maurer Wagner

IRENE'S GERMAN POTATO SALAD

6-8 large potatoes (thin skinned white or red are best)	½ cup corn or canola and some olive oil (mixed)
1 large red onion	1 Tbsp sugar
3-4 large sweet sour pickles	1 tsp garlic powder
½ cup wine vinegar	1 Tbsp Dijon mustard (optional)
¼ cup water	1 Tbsp salt
	pepper

Wash, peel and slice raw potatoes into thin slices, not more than ¼ inch. Place into slow boiling water and cook until just done. (check frequently) Drain, let cool well. You can also cook the potatoes whole and slice them after they are well cooled, best overnight. Chop the red onion fine. Cut pickles into small cubes. Make vinaigrette and pour over cooled potatoes, mix slowly and carefully, so you don't get mashed potatoes. Let marinate for ½ hour. If there is too much liquid, drain some of it off, so the salad does not become too soggy! Serves 6.

Irene Seeland

MARTINE'S POTATO SALAD

⅓ cup Italian salad dressing
7 medium potatoes, cooked
   in skins
¾ cup celery, sliced

⅓ cup green onions, sliced
4 hard boiled eggs
½ cup sour cream
1 cup mayonnaise

Peel potatoes and slice. Pour Italian salad dressing over warm potatoes. Chill for at least 2 hours. Add celery and onions. Chop egg whites and add. Save yolks. Mix yolks with mayonnaise and sour cream and fold mixture into the salad. Chill for 2 hours. Makes 8 servings.

Martine Kreiger

POTATO SALAD

4 lbs. small, evenly sized
   potatoes
2 egg yolks
oil
salt to taste
freshly ground pepper to
   taste

sugar to taste
1 onion, medium to large
cider vinegar or juice from
   dill pickles
3-4 dill pickles, not garlic
¼ c. chopped parsley

1. Boil potatoes in their jackets, peel and slice them.
2. In food processor, mix egg yolks adding oil until thick, but not as thick as mayonnaise. Finely chop onion and incorporate, along with vinegar or pickle juice, salt, pepper and sugar. Season on the strong side since the potatoes will absorb flavors. Pour over warm sliced potatoes, liquid should cover them.
3. Add 3-4 pickles, chopped, and parsley. Mix all together and cover, place in refrigerator and allow to soak for several hours. Taste and adjust seasonings.
4. An alternate method substitutes commercial mayonnaise (Hellmann's) for the egg yolks and oil. Add other ingredients and pour over the sliced, fully cooled potatoes.

Leni Kroul

GRILLED CHICKEN PASTA SALAD

1 lb rotini pasta
2 lbs grilled chicken cutlets
  or boneless breasts cut
  into bite sized pieces
1 large sweet red pepper,
  cored, seeded and diced
1 large green pepper, cored,
  seeded and diced
1 medium red onion, halved
  and thinly sliced
2 scallions, trimmed and
  thinly sliced

2 Tbsp minced fresh dill
1 cup light mayonnaise
½ cup honey
1 tsp prepared mustard
1 tsp sugar
1 tsp onion powder
1 tsp dried parsley flakes
¼ tsp salt
¼ tsp black pepper
½ cup canola or vegetable
  oil

Cook pasta following package directions. When cool mix with chicken in a large bowl. Added peppers, onion, scallions and dill. In a medium bowl, whisk mayonnaise, vinegar, honey, mustard, sugar, onion powder, parsley flakes, salt and pepper. Gradually whisk in the oil. Pour mayonnaise mixture over pasta and chicken and toss. Refrigerate until ready to serve.

Anonymous

It's the dill and the dressing that make this salad soooo good. And this recipe makes plenty, for a sit down meal for eight or to nibble on all week long.

TORTELLINI SALAD

1 lb. stuffed tortellini
  (cheese or mushroom)
8 oz. sun-dried tomatoes
½ cup olive oil
1 Tbsp lemon juice
2 garlic cloves (pressed)

1 Tbsp pepper
1 Tbsp salt
2 small. jars artichokes
½ cup pine nuts
½ cup dried parsley
2 tsp basil

Cook tortellini as directed. Mix tortellini, sun-dried tomatoes, olive oil, lemon juice, garlic, salt and pepper. Add artichokes, pine nuts, parsley and basil. Chill, if desired, sprinkle with parmesan cheese before serving.

Sushma Krishna

APPLE, CARROT AND RAISIN SALAD

2 oz. raisins
½ c. orange juice
1 lb. carrots, shredded
1 lb. apples (Golden
  Delicious or Granny
  Smith), shredded

1 oz. horseradish, shredded
  fresh or bottled (drained)
3 oz. vegetable oil
salt, to taste
freshly ground pepper, to
  taste

1. Combine the raisins and orange juice; let raisins become plump. Drain raisins and reserve the orange juice.
2. Combine raisins, carrots, apples and horseradish.
3. Mix together reserved orange juice, oil, salt and pepper. Add to shredded vegetables and combine all thoroughly.

Mary Kroul McAlpin

This recipe multiplies and keeps well, so it's great for parties or for big batches when you don't want to cook every day. Originally from a CIA cookbook.

FRAN BEACH'S FRUIT SALAD

1 cup mandarin orange
  sections
1 cup pineapple chunks
1 cup coconut

1 cup tiny marshmallows
1 cup sour cream
Nuts if desired.

Mix and chill.

Hattie Grifo
in memory of my Godmother, Fran Beach

* * * * *

It is odd how all men develop the notion, as they grow older, that their mothers were wonderful cooks. I have yet to meet a man who will admit that his mother was a kitchen assassin and nearly poisoned him.

Robertson Davies, Canadian Author

YOUR FAVORITE RECIPES

Recipe   Page Number

SOUPS & SALADS

Roses on the table
Austa Densmore Sturdevant (1855-1936)

Recipe Favorites

Page No.

Recipe Title:_____ _____

_____ _____

_____ _____

_____ _____

_____ _____

_____ _____

_____ _____

_____ _____

_____ _____

_____ _____

Family Favorites

Page No.

Recipe Title:_____ _____

_____ _____

_____ _____

_____ _____

_____ _____

_____ _____

Notes:_____

_____

_____

_____

702-08

MAIN DISHES

BIRD'S FAVORITE CHICKEN PIE

1 3-4 lb. chicken	bay leaf
3 medium potatoes	flour (or rice &/or tapioca
peas	flour)*
salt	chicken gravy
Herbamare (optional)	pastry crust

Put the chicken in a large pot, add bay leaf, and cover with cold water. Bring to a boil, then simmer til tender, about 45 minutes or more. When done, lift chicken into a colander set over a bowl (to catch the juices), to cool. You can use the broth for soup. While the chicken is cooking, make the pastry dough (see below), wrap it in plastic wrap and refrigerate. To make gravy, skim some of the fat off the chicken broth, plus some of the broth (about 1-2 c together), and put in a saute pan or cast iron fry pan; heat. When the mixture is bubbling, whisk in approximately. 1-2 tablespoons flour; as the mixture thickens, increase the amount of gravy by adding broth, then cooking down to thicken; repeat until you have enough made to nearly cover the ingredients when they are in the pie pan (2-3 cups). Season with salt.

When chicken is cool, pick the meat off the bones and put in large bowl. Peel the potatoes and cut into 1" cubes, put in the bowl with the chicken, add about ½ lb. peas, fresh or frozen. Stir and season with salt, Herbamare, or your favorite seasoning.

Cut your pastry dough in half and roll a bottom crust on a floured wood or marble surface, place in a 9 or 10" pie pan. Put meat, potato, and pea mixture in the crust, and pour in the gravy. Roll out the second half of the crust and put it over the top, trim, brush the edge of the bottom crust with water, and crimp the edges of the two crusts together. Cut several slits in the top to allow steam to escape. Bake at 450° for 15 min., reduce heat to 350° and bake for about 40 more minutes or until the crust is golden brown. Let sit about 15 minutes before serving.

Plain Pastry for Crust:

2 cups flour
½ t salt

⅔ c cold butter
Ice water (about ⅓ c)

Easiest to do in a food processor. Mix flour and salt in processor bowl. Cut butter into chunks and drop into bowl, evenly spaced around on top of the flour. Pulse the mixture til the butter is mixed into flour, with chunks no bigger than peas. Then blend as you pour the ice water in slowly, til dough is soft and rollable but not too wet. Cool in the refrigerator as above, until ready to use.

John "Bird" Wende

Herbamare is an herbal and sea salt mixture available at health food stores.

*For those who can't eat wheat/gluten, make the gravy with rice and/or tapioca flour, bake and serve without a crust.

APRICOT CHICKEN

6 boneless, skinless chicken
  breasts
1 envelope dry Onion Soup
  Mix

1 8-11 oz. jar Apricot Jam
8 oz. French dressing

Mix all and spread over chicken breasts. Bake at 350°F for 45 minutes to 1 hour. Serves 6.

Joyce Stedner

* * * * *

No one who cooks, cooks alone. Even at her most solitary, a cook in the kitchen is surrounded by generations of cooks past, the advice and menus of cooks present, the wisdom of cookbook writers.

Laurie Colwin

ROADKILL CHICKEN

(Craig Claiborne's Mother's Smothered Chicken)

1 3½ lb. chicken, butterflied (split down the backbone, breast left intact and unsplit)
Salt to taste
Freshly ground pepper to taste

pinch thyme or herbes de Provence (optional)
2 Tbsp. butter
2 Tbsp. flour
1 ½ c. chicken stock (or use part white wine)

1. A black cast iron frying pan is essential for this dish. Sprinkle the chicken on both sides with salt and pepper. Select a pan large enough to hold the chicken comfortably when it is spread out as if for broiling. Fold the chicken wings under to hold them securely.
2. Melt the butter in the pan and add the chicken, skin-side down. Cover the chicken firmly with a plate the fits comfortably inside the pan. Add several weights, about 5 pounds, on top of the plate. Cook over low heat, checking the skin of the chicken, for about 25 minutes, until it is nicely browned. With tongs and a wide spatula, turn chicken skin-side up, replace plate and weights and continue cooking 15 minutes.
3. Remove chicken and pour off all but 2 Tbsp. fat from the frying pan. Add the flour and incorporate with wire whip. Add stock gradually with optional herbs and blend; when thickened, return the chicken to the pan, skin-side up. Cover again with plate and weights and continue cooking over low heat about 30 minutes longer, until chicken is exceptionally tender. Spoon sauce over.
4. Cut the chicken into serving pieces and serve with sauce and fluffy rice.

Mary Kroul McAlpin

This was published in the NY Times Magazine in the mid 1970s. I've never seen it anywhere since, but it's long been a favorite in our family; it truly deserves memorializing.

CHEESY CHICKEN

3 whole chicken breasts,
  skinned and cut into small
  pieces
1 clove garlic, minced
½ cup melted butter or
  margarine

½ cup fine dry bread crumbs
¼ cup grated sharp cheddar
  cheese
2 Tbsp grated parmesan
  cheese
salt and pepper to taste

Add garlic to melted butter and let stand 20 minutes. Mix together bread crumbs and cheeses. Salt and pepper the chicken and dip in melted garlic butter, then into crumb mixture.

Place in 9x13 inch baking dish. Pour remaining butter over chicken. Bake uncovered in a 350°F oven for 30-40 minutes. Serves 6.

Audrey Keir

* * * * *

I don't think a really good pie can be made without a dozen or so children peeking over your shoulder as you stoop to look at it every little while.

John Gould

TUSCAN CHICKEN

1 whole chicken
2 Lg Cans whole or diced
  tomatoes
1 large onion cut in slices
  from the root to the top
4 cloves of garlic, peeled and
  coarsely chopped
½ lb. button mushrooms,
  cleaned

1 can whole artichokes cut
  into quarters
1 cup pitted kalamata olives
2 T Olive oil
Salt and pepper
1 bunch Fresh Basil ½ cup
  finely chopped and the
  rest for garnish

Turn the oven on to 400. Clean the chicken and cut off excess fat, set aside. Mix the basil and garlic with olive oil. Season with Salt and Pepper.

Massage into the chicken. ON the stove top heat the roasting pan and add the tomatoes, onions, mushrooms and artichoke bring to a simmer. Place the chicken on the top and move the pan to the oven. Turn the oven down to 350. Bake for about an hour until the temperature in the breast is 160-170 degrees. The chicken will still cook after it is taken out of the oven.

Ingredients can be substituted to make this your own changing this every time you make it.

You can use:

Red and or yellow peppers
Zucchini
Eggplant
White beans

Capers
Nuts
Raisins

You can change the herb from basil to thyme, rosemary tarragon.

Lee Ann Leichtfuss

* * * * *

You cannot sell a blemished apple in the supermarket, but you can sell a tasteless one provided it is shiny, smooth, even, uniform and bright.

Elspeth Huxley

COUNTRY FRENCH CASSOULET

1 lb hot or mild, fresh Italian sausage, bias sliced into ½ inch pieces

1 lb boneless skinless chicken breasts, cut into ½ inch strips

½ cup chopped onion, fresh or frozen

2 19 oz. cans of cannelloni beans, drained and rinsed

2 cups coarsely chopped escarole or spinach (baby is best)

¾ cups of reduced sodium chicken broth

¼ cup of dry white wine or increase broth to 1 cup

2 Tbsp fresh thyme or 1 tsp dried

¼ cup grated parmesan cheese

If you like add a pinch of this or that: crushed garlic, black pepper, salt, button mushrooms, coarsely chopped parsley, rosemary or crushed red pepper.

Cook sausage and onion about 10 minutes, drain off excess fat. Remove from pan and saute chicken breasts about 8 minutes. Add beans, broth, wine, thyme and bring to a boil. Reduce heat, cover and simmer 5 minutes. Ladle into serving bowls and sprinkle with parmesan cheese. Can be served over penne or a similar pasta. Serve with a mixed green salad dressed with oil and vinegar and a warm French baguette. Close your eyes, hum.... you're in the French countryside, yes, yes.

Tom Bolger

Traditionally made in the southwest of France, this dish is made with duck or goose, sausage, roast pork, and white beans and can take hours to days to prepare.

* * * * *

When we lose, I eat. When we win, I eat. I also eat when we're rained out.

Tommy Lasorda
(Dodgers Baseball Team Manager)

CHICKEN MASON

1 3 ½ lb chicken
1 Tbsp Olive Oil
1 Tbsp Butter
8 ea Medium Mushrooms
8 ea Lg. Cloves Garlic
1 ½ C Chopped onions

12 ea Baby carrots
¾ tsp Salt
½ tsp Black pepper
1 C Frozen Peas
Chives to garnish

Sauté chicken in oil & butter for 8 to 10 min until brown; remove breasts. Add mushrooms & garlic & onions simmer 2 minutes. Add carrots, salt & pepper, wine; bring to boil simmer 10 to 12 minutes. Return breasts simmer for 5 more minutes. Add peas simmer 3 more minutes. Sprinkle chives over chicken and serve.

Jim McKenney

CHICKEN DIVAN

6 chicken breasts, cooked, sliced
2 boxed pkg frozen broccoli, cooked
1 can cream of mushroom soup

1 can cream of chicken soup
2 Tbsp Worcestershire sauce
2 Tbsp cooking Sherry
grated cheese
salt and pepper

Layer bottom of baking dish with broccoli. Put chicken on top. Mix soups, sherry and Worcestershire to make a sauce. Pour over chicken and broccoli. Top with grated cheese. Bake at 350°F for 30 minutes.

Anonymous

* * * * *

What will be the death of me are buillabaisses, food spiced with pimiento, shellfish, and a load of exquisite rubbish which I eat in disproportionate quantities.
Emile Zola, French Writer (1840-1902)

CHICKEN CURRY

Medium pkg chicken (breast,
  thighs or drumsticks)
3 Tbsp olive oil
2-3 medium yellow onions,
  medium
2 sq inches of ginger, grated
2 large garlic cloves,
  chopped

1 Tbsp chili powder
pinch turmeric
¼ tsp salt
1 tsp cumin
1 tsp coriander
¼ tsp garam masala (all
  spice)

If using chicken breast, cut into cubes and set aside.
Heat oil on low/medium heat. Add chopped onions and fry
until glistening. Add all garlic and ginger and fry for 2 minutes. Add rest of ingredients except chicken and mix. Add
chicken and mix well. Cover and cook for about 1 hour mixing occasionally, until chicken is completely cooked.

Sindu Krishna

INDIAN SPICED CHICKEN

4 Chicken legs, split and
  skinless
4 garlic cloves minced
2 T ground coriander
2 T curry powder
1 T fennel seeds
1 T crushed red pepper
2 T grated ginger

1 t cardamom
1 large baking potato, large
  diced
3 carrots sliced large
2 C water
1 bunch collard greens
2 T sugar
4 T tomato paste

Mix together all the spices and toss in the chicken to
coat. In a large deep pan brown the chicken pieces add the
remaining spices if any are left. Add the carrots, potatoes,
water, tomato paste and sugar and simmer for 30 minutes.
Add the collard greens and continue to simmer for 15
minutes.

Lee Ann Leichtfuss

* * * * *

Only the pure of heart can make a good soup.
Ludwig Van Beethoven

HATTIE'S CHICKEN IN A POT

1 3-4 lb chicken
10 or so shallots
12 +/- Brussels sprouts
2 large sweet potatoes
1 head broccoflower or
   cauliflower (white, orange
   or purple)
4 or 5 carrots, cut in
   diagonal slices
1 pkg babybella mushrooms

1 onion
1 garlic clove, whole
1 or 2 garlic cloves, mashed
   in a press
Olive oil
salt & pepper to taste
Herbamare, if have it
tarragon or other herbs to
   your taste
Bay leaf if liked.

Rinse and dry chicken, salt the cavity and insert peeled onion and whole garlic clove. Truss and put in a 7.5 qt. or larger, Le Cruset or similar pot. Peel shallots and put in very large bowl, cut in half if large. Clean and trim the Brussels sprout. Wash, peel, and cut the sweet potatoes into 2 inch wedges. Wash and cut up the broccoli or cauliflower into florets. Wash and slice the carrots, slice on a diagonal. Clean the mushrooms, trim stem ends, and quarter or halve, depending on size. Put all these ingredients into the large bowl with the shallots. Add the mashed garlic cloves. Pour about ¼ c olive oil over the mixture of vegetables, and stir them well with a large spoonula or similar utensil. Add salt, pepper (if liked), and Herbamare (optional if you don't have it), and any herbs you care to add, and stir the mixture some more. Add a bit more oil as/if necessary, to moisten the veggies. Pour/spoon the vegetables around and over the chicken. Sprigs of tarragon can be placed over the mixture. A bay leaf or two can be tucked into the vegetables. Cover, and cook in a 400°F oven for 1 ½ to 2 hours, depending on your oven and size of chicken. Check for doneness with an instant read thermometer.

Hattie Grifo

When chicken is done, transfer it to a platter and let it rest 10-15 mins. before carving. Serve the vegetables from the pot, or transfer to a large serving bowl. There will be a wonderful, tasty broth that can be ladled over the chicken and vegetables when served.

PEPPER CHICKEN PASTA

2 lbs chopped boneless
   chicken breast
5-6 red and green bell
   peppers, chopped
12 cloves garlic, crushed
2 28 oz cans diced tomatoes
2 Tbsp flour

1 quart heavy cream
2 oz. hot sauce
olive oil
oregano
Parmesan cheese
pasta

In skillet or wok, cook chopped peppers and garlic in olive oil until soft. In separate sauce pot, heat diced tomatoes and oregano stirring occasionally over medium heat. Let tomatoes cook down. Add cooked peppers and hot sauce to tomato pot. In skillet or wok, cook chicken thoroughly in oil and add to tomatoes. Continue to simmer tomato pot without lid. Heat water to boiling for pasta. In the skillet, heat heavy cream on low heat with flour till thick. Add 2-4 oz. parmesan cheese. Add cream mixture to tomato pot during last half hour of cooking. Pour over pasta, add parmesan cheese.

Greg Marl

Total cooking time from begining will be about 2 hours.

* * * * *

The smell of good bread baking, like the sound of lightly flowing water, is indescribable in its evocation of innocence and delight.

M. F. K. Fisher

CHICKEN QUESADILLA

2 pieces of chicken breast
(can substitute steak, black
beans, and corn)
1 medium/large green
peppers
1 medium/large red pepper
red or white onion
8 inch tortillas

shredded cheese (sharp
cheddar, Monterey Jack)
juice of 2-3 limes
oregano
basil
cinnamon
salt and pepper
chili powder to taste

Prepare in a bowl large enough to hold the following ingredients: juice of 2-3 limes, about ½ tsp oregano and basil, pinch of cinnamon, crushed black pepper, pinch of salt and chili powder as desired. Mix together and set aside. Add chicken breast to boiling water and cook for about 7 minutes or until cooked through. Shred the chicken using two forks. Smaller pieces will fit better. Put chicken in lime juice mixture. Cut peppers and onion. Steam in a pan with a small amount of water for about 4 minutes or until desired tenderness. Combine with chicken in lime juice. You can use either a non-stick pan, stainless steel with a small amount of oil, or else a grill such as a Foreman grill. Preheat the grill or pan that you are using. Put cheese on half of the tortilla, then place chicken and vegetable mixture on top. Be sure not to make it too full so that it is easy to flip. Cook each side of the quesadilla until both sides are brown, about 2-3 minutes in a pan and 6 minutes total in a Foreman grill. Be sure the cheese is melted. Cut into thirds and serve with hot sauce, salsa, guacamole or whatever you are in the mood for!

Andrea Kreiger

* * * * *

I understand the big food companies are developing a tearless onion. I think they can do it after all, they've already given us tasteless bread.

Robert Orben

ELLA'S BAKED CHICKEN

3 c Corn flake crumbs
½ tsp paprika
¼ tsp salt
⅛ tsp pepper
½ tsp garlic powder or onion
   powder

1 c fresh parley chopped fine
4 lbs Chicken (whichever
   parts you prefer)
Milk or half & half
Butter

Wash & dry chicken parts. Either buy a box of Corn Flake Crumbs or crush till fine enough corn flakes for 3 cups.

Mix all dry ingredients together very well and put half in a large baggie. Put 2 or 3 inches of milk or half & half in a shallow bowl. Dip chicken in milk then drop into the baggie and completely coat. Move coated chicken to a baking pan and top each piece with a little dab of butter. Continue replenishing corn flake mixture and milk as needed until all the chicken is coated and on the baking pan. Bake at 350 for approximately 35 minutes.

The times will vary depending on your choice of chicken pieces.

Mary Ann Maurer

I have modified this recipe that originally came from Ella Stedner, our former Library Director. It was used for the Library Day chicken dinner.

* * * * *

The most remarkable thing about my mother is that for 30 years she served the family nothing but leftovers. The original meal has never been found.

Calvin Trillin

JEFF'S CHICKEN PICATTA

4 skinless boneless chicken
  breast halves (cut into 1-2
  inch chunks)
1 Tbsp butter, room
  temperature
¼ cup all purpose flour
Additional 1 ½ Tbsp all
  purpose flour
¼ cup seasoned bread
  crumbs
4 Tbsp olive oil
1 cup dry white wine

¼ - ½ cup fresh lemon juice
1 cup low-salt fat-free
  chicken broth
½ cup slightly drained
  capers
1- 1 ½ cups fresh parsley
¾ lb crimini mushrooms,
  very thinly sliced
1 lg yellow onion, very thinly
  sliced
1 pkg (12-16 oz.) yolk-less
  egg noodles

In a plastic bag, sprinkle chicken with a few Tbsp each of oil, lemon juice, and wine. Set aside. Mix 1 Tbsp butter and 1 ½ Tbsp flour in a small bowl until smooth. Set aside. Chop parsley, slice mushrooms and onions. Place ¼ cup flour and bread crumbs in another plastic bag. Add chicken and shake to coat. (for an even lower fat version omit bread crumbs, coat chicken very lightly with flour only and substitute non-stick cooking spray for oil.) Cook noodles.

While noodles are cooking, heat 1 Tbsp oil in large skillet. Add chicken and cook until pieces are browned and cooked through. Transfer chicken to platter; tent with foil to keep warm. Add remaining oil to skillet and saute mushrooms and onions until soft.

Add wine, lemon juice and broth and bring to a boil. Whisk in butter-flour mixture and boil until sauce thickens slightly. Stir in chicken, capers, parsley and drained noodles. Heat through and serve. (Chicken mixture could also be served atop the noodles; rice or couscous could be substituted. Makes 4 servings.

Jeff Woodman

* * * * *

Of soup and love, the first is best.
Spanish Proverb

OPEN-FACED CHICKEN SANDWICHES

4 English muffins, sliced
2 10 oz. cans breast of
  chicken, drained
2 medium tomatoes, sliced

8 slices American cheese
1 can Cream of Chicken
  soup

    Slice English muffins in half and place on a cookie sheet or broiler pan. On each half put pieces of chicken. Spoon soup over the chicken. Add a slice of tomato and a slice of cheese to each sandwich. Place pan of sandwiched under a preheated boiler until everything is hot and bubbly. Serve hot.

Judy Rode

* * * * *

One morning, as I went to the freezer door, I asked my wife, 'What should I take out for dinner?' Without a moment's hesitation, she replied, 'Me.'

Anonymous

TURKEY SAUSAGE-SPINACH LASAGNA WITH SPICY TOMATO SAUCE

Lasagna:

1 Tbsp olive oil
1 ¼ lbs. hot Italian turkey sausage, casings removed
1 15 oz. container ricotta cheese
1 10 oz. package frozen chopped spinach, thawed and squeezed dry
1 ¾ cups grated parmesan cheese

2 large eggs
3 Tbsp whipping cream
½ tsp dried basil
½ tsp dried oregano
½ tsp ground black pepper
9 uncooked lasagna noodles
3 cups shredded Provolone cheese (12 oz.)
Spicy Tomato Sauce

Heat oil in a large skillet over medium heat. Add sausages, saute until brown, using fork to break up meat into coarse pieces, about 7 minutes. Add Spicy Tomato Sauce, simmer 5 minutes.

Position rack in the center of oven; preheat to 375°F. Whisk ricotta, spinach, 1 cup parmesan, eggs, cream, basil, oregano, and pepper in large bowl. Set aside. Spoon 1 cup sauce over bottom of 12x9x2 in. class baking dish. Place 3 noodles over sauce in single layer. Spread 1 cup sauce over noodles. Spoon 1 cup ricotta mixture over sauce. Sprinkle ¼ cup parmesan and 1 cup Provolone over ricotta mixture. Repeat layering with 3 noodle, 1 cup sauce, 1 cup ricotta mixture, ¼ cup parmesan and 1 cup Provolone. Arrange remaining 3 noodles over cheese. Spoon 1 cup sauce over noodles and sprinkle with remaining ¼ cup parmesan and 1 cup Provolone. Dollop remaining ricotta mixture atop lasagna. Spoon 2 ½ cups sauce around ricotta dollops. Tightly cover baking dish with foil.

Bake lasagna for 50 minutes; uncover and continue baking until noodles are tender and lasagna is hot and bubbly, about 25 minutes longer. Let lasagna stand 15 minute before serving.

Can be prepared 1 day ahead. Cool slightly. Cover and refrigerate. Re-warm, covered with foil, in 350°F oven about 45 minutes. Re-warm sauce in a small pan over medium heat. Serve lasagna, passing remaining sauce.

Spicy Tomato Sauce:

3 Tbsp olive oil
1 medium onion, finely
 chopped
6 cloves garlic, minced
1 tsp dried oregano
¾ tsp dried basil
¾ tsp dried marjoram

¾ tsp crushed red pepper
2 28 oz. cans Italian style
 tomatoes
1 cup canned crushed
 tomatoes with added puree
½ cup dry red wine

Heat oil in large heavy saucepan over medium heat. Add onion, garlic, oregano, basil, marjoram, and crushed red pepper. Cover and cook until onion is translucent, stirring occasionally, about 10 minutes. Add remaining ingredients, simmer gently, uncovered, until sauce thickens and measures 8 cups total, breaking up tomatoes with spoon and stirring occasionally, about 1 hour 15 minutes. Season sauce to taste with salt and pepper. Makes 8 cups.

Linda Rogers

One great thing about this lasagna is that the noodles don't need to be pre-boiled. The dish has a lot of liquid (in the form of sauce) and goes in to the oven covered, so the noodles cook perfectly.

* * * * *

You can say this for ready-mixes -- the next generation isn't going to have any trouble making pies exactly like mother used to make.

Earl Wilson

JEFF'S WAAAY LOWFAT TURKEY MEATLOAF

Turkey Meatloaf:

2 pkgs (approx. 2 lbs) extra lean 97% fat free ground turkey
2-3 tbls olive oil
2 large green bell peppers, finely diced
12-16 oz. mushrooms, finely diced
1 large spanish onion, finely diced
8 oz. reduced fat/fat-free sharp cheddar, grated or finely diced
¾- 1 cup grated Parmigiano Reggiano cheese
1 ½- 2 cups season Italian breadcrumbs
3- 4 tbsp Worcestershire sauce
3- 4 tbsp light soy sauce
2 large eggs, beaten (or 4 whites, or Egg Beater equivalent)
1 tbsp dried oregano
¾ tbsp dried basil
½ tbsp each dried tarragon, garlic powder and ground black pepper

Saute the 3 veggies in the oil until soft and completely shrunken. Add the 5 spices and saute another 5 minutes or so. Allow to cool, then mix with turkey, cheeses, Worcestershire, 2 tbsp of the soy and the eggs. Mix thoroughly, then add bread crumbs to desired consistency (should hold together in a fairly tight ball like any meatloaf). Shape into 2 loaves, brush with remaining soy sauce (to better brown them) and bake in a 350°F oven for 45- 50 minutes. Serve with Katie's sauce.

Katie's Sauce:

1 cup ketchup
3- 4 tbsp vinegar
⅓- ½ cup diced sweet pickles
⅓ cup diced onion (optional)
splash of red wine (optional)

Combine all ingredients in a small saucepan and simmer over medium heat until heated through.

Jeff Woodman

STEDNER'S CHILI CON CARNE

1 lb ground beef
1 cup chopped onions
2 cloves garlic, minced
1 Tbsp oil
2-3 tsp chili powder
½ tsp salt

dash pepper (calls for a dash of cayenne pepper, but I never use it)
1 1 lb can tomatoes
2-3 1 lb cans kidney beans, undrained
1 1 lb can tomato sauce or puree

In large skillet, add oil and cook ground beef with onions, garlic and spices. Cook meat until brown and add tomatoes, sauce and kidney beans. Cover and cook over low heat about 45 minutes. Stir now and then. Uncover and cook to desired consistency.

Joyce Stedner

CHILI CORN CASSEROLE

1 dozen eggs (beaten)
4 cups (2 pkgs) Mexican Taco Shredded Cheese
2 cans creamed corn

1 jar hot or medium salsa
2 4 oz. cans chopped green chilies

Mix all ingredients together in a large Pyrex casserole. Bake at 325°F for 45 min. the bake at 350°F for an additional 15 minutes.

Deena Davidson

* * * * *

My kids always perceived the bathroom as a place where you wait it out until all the groceries are unloaded from the car.

Erma Bombeck

JEFF'S VIRTUALLY FAT FREE CHILI

2- 3 Tbsp olive oil (this is the only fat)
2 large green bell peppers
2 lbs. mushrooms
2 large Spanish onions
6 15.5 oz. cans of beans rinsed (2 each: red kidney, pinto and black beans)
1 12- 16 oz. bag frozen peas (soybeans can be substituted)
1 12- 16 oz. bag frozen corn

2- 3 large cans crushed tomatoes (and/or tomato puree)
2 pkg chili seasoning (plus chili powder, cumin, red pepper flakes, and garlic powder to taste)
1 Tbsp ground black pepper
4- 5 Tbsp Worcestershire sauce
1 six-pack your favorite beer (the darker, the better)

Roughly chop the first three veggies and saute in the oil (peppers first, and when they begin to soften add the mushrooms and onion) in a big (preferably non-stick) pot until the mushrooms begin to give off their liquid. Add the spices, 1 can of tomatoes, Worcestershire sauce and a beer. Simmer, stirring frequently for 30 minutes or longer. (the longer and more slowly this cooks- the better it gets) Add the beans, more tomatoes and another beer. Reduce heat to low and simmer as long as possible, (all day) adding more beer as liquid reduces. Add more beer and/or tomatoes as needed for desired consistency (simmer for as long as somebody is around to stir it) Half and hour before removing from heat add peas and corn.

For chili con carne add 1 ½ lbs ground lean turkey to sauteing veggies.

Serve over rice with shredded low fat or fat free cheddar and diced raw onion (add low fat or fat free sour cream or yogurt if desired).

This freezes really well and defrosts in the microwave quickly. Served over a microwave-baked potato this makes a fast, filling, fat free lunch.

Jeff Woodman

MEAT LOAF

3 lb. meat loaf mixture
4 slices bread, softened in
  milk
3 eggs
1 clove garlic, minced or
  pressed
salt to taste
freshly ground pepper to
  taste
about 1 tsp. chicken stock
  base, or some leftover
  gravy

bacon slices
2 onions, chopped
2 stalks celery, chopped
1 can mushrooms, drained
pinch of thyme
oregano to taste
2-3 Tbsp. chopped fresh
  parsley
1 large can tomatoes
1 8 oz. can tomato sauce
4 tsp. chicken stock base

1. Oven at 450°F.
2. Mix meat, softened bread, eggs, garlic, salt, pepper, 1 tsp. stock base or leftover gravy. If necessary, add more milk (or powdered milk and water) to make a rather loose mixture. Form into a loaf in a large baking pan. Cover with bacon strips.
3. Place in oven and roast until bacon is well browned.
4. Oven at 375°F.
5. Remove meatloaf from oven and add rest of ingredients. Cover loosely with aluminum foil. Roast until vegetables are soft (time can vary with stove and altitude).
6. Serve on platter, with some sauce spooned over and some on the side, accompanied by baked potatoes.

Leni Kroul

Leni's invention and a family classic. Recipe doubles easily, and leftovers can be turned into meat "cubes" in spaghetti sauce.

* * * * *

We are living in a world today where lemonade is made from artificial flavors and furniture polish is made from real lemons.

Alfred E. Newman

BEEF STUFFED SQUARES

(Meatloaf)

8 oz. package herb-seasoned
 stuffing mix
1 C. tomato juice
2 eggs, beaten separately
2 lb ground chuck

1 envelope onion soup mix
2 T butter
13 oz. can sliced mushrooms,
 drained (reserve liquid)

In large bowl place 1C stuffing mix; add 1 C tomato juice, 1 beaten egg, 2# chuck, 1 envelope onion soup mix. Thoroughly combine. Preheat oven to 375. Put chuck mixture into 9x9x2 baking dish. In 2T hot butter in skillet saute 13 oz. sliced mushrooms drained. In bowl place rest of stuffing mix, add 1 beaten egg, mushroom liquid and hot water to make 1 C. Add sauteed mushrooms and mix well. Pat on top of chuck mixture. Bake 40-45 minutes. Allow to cool slightly and cut into squares.

Ruth Diem

SUE'S CABBAGE

1 small/medium head of
 cabbage
1 ½ lbs. ground turkey and
 ground beef
2 Vidalia onions,
 sliced/quartered (Not
 diced)

2 cans Campbell's tomato
 bisque soup
little milk
1 can of fat-free/low sodium
 chicken broth
Mrs. Dash seasoning
cooked rice or flat noodles

In a very large frying pan, pour in the can of broth. Slice and quarter onions, shred cabbage and then put all in the frying pan with broth. Sprinkle contents with Mrs. Dash. Bring mixture to a boil, reduce heat, and cook 30-45 minutes, mixing until onions and cabbage are fully cooked. While this is cooking, in a separate frying pan, cook meat. When cabbage is soft, add 2 cans of tomato bisque along with meat and cook altogether for at least 5 minutes. Add a little milk if you want more sauce. Serve over hot rice or pasta.

Paula Medley

HAMBURGER WITH CREAM-COGNAC SAUCE

¼ hamburger
Dijon mustard
1 tsp butter

2 Tbsp cream
1 Tbsp cognac
pepper to taste

Make a patty and brush both sides with mustard. Saute patty on both sides (7 minutes each side for rare). Remove burger to warm plate; reserving brown bits. Return pan to heat and add cream and cognac, stirring constantly until sauce thickens. Makes 1 serving.

Amy Polk

* * * * *

The only way to keep your health is to eat what you don't want, drink what you don't like, and do what you'd rather not.

Mark Twain

GAME SHEPHERD'S PIE

(adapted from Nigella Lawson)

1 oz dried porcini
  mushrooms (do NOT
  substitute)
1 cup boiling water
2 onions, chopped
2 carrots, chopped
2 cloves garlic, chopped
2-3 Tbsp olive oil
½ lb button mushrooms
1 lb ground venison (or
  other game meat)
1 lb ground pork
1 Tbsp flour

1 14 oz can chopped
  tomatoes
1 Tbsp tomato paste, diluted
  in ½ cup water
⅙ cup Marsala wine
Worcestershire sauce, a few
  drops
4 ½ lbs potatoes
1 ½ lbs parsnips
butter and milk to mash
  potatoes and parsnips
butter (to dot pie before
  baking)

Pans needed: 9x13 inch pan and Dutch oven. Preheat oven to 425°F. Pour 1 cup boiling water over the porcini mushrooms and let them steep about 20 minutes. Drain the mushrooms and reserve the liquid. Coarsely chop porcinis. Saute onions, carrots and garlic in olive oil for about 10 minutes in the Dutch oven. Add porcini and button mushrooms and saute about 5 minutes. Set mixture aside in a bowl. Next, saute the venison and pork in the Dutch oven (add a little more oil, if needed). Salt to taste. When there is no pink left in the meat, add the vegetable/mushroom mixture back into the pot. Stir in the reserves porcini liquid, tomatoes, tomato paste mixture, Marsala wine and a few drops of Worcestershire sauce. Simmer on low for 1 hour (more if desired). In the meantime, boil together the potatoes and the parsnips until soft and mash with the butter and milk. Set aside. After simmering the meat mixture, taste and season with salt and pepper, as needed. Add the meat mixture to the 9x13 pan. Spread the mashed mixture on top, sealing the edges of the pan to prevent juices from bubbling up. Score the potatoes with a fork to create fine lines. Dot the top with butter. Bake for 10-15 minutes in 425°F oven. This recipe can be made ahead of time. Simply prepare as above, but do not bake. Refrigerate until ready, and then place in a 375°F oven for 1 hour.

Becky McDevitt

Please do not substitute the dried porcinis- they add a delicious smoky flavor to the pie.

SAUERBRATEN

Meat:

4 lbs beef rump (venison can also be used)
2 medium onions, cut into chunks
½ lemon, sliced
2 ½ cups water
1 ½ cups red wine vinegar
12 whole cloves
6 bay leaves
6 whole peppercorns
1 Tbsp sugar
1 Tbsp salt
¼ tsp ginger

Put all ingredients together in a large pot, cover and refrigerate for at least 36 hours, or as long as 3-4 days. Make sure to turn daily. After marinating, remove the meat and wipe dry. Strain liquid making sure to remove all solids. Brown meat in a large saucepan. Add strained liquid, cover and cook slowly for 2 hours or until tender. When meat is finished remove and cover with a tin foil tent to keep warm. Make gravy with remaining liquid. Serve with spatzle.

* * * * *

It would be nice if the Food and Drug Administration stopped issuing warnings about toxic substances and just gave me the names of one or two things still safe to eat.
Robert Fuoss

Gravy:

For each cup of gravy desired combine:

¾ cup meat juices   ⅓ cup crushed gingersnaps
¼ cup water

Mix ingredients together in a saucepan. Cook and stir until thick enough to be a gravy. Pour over top of sliced Sauerbraten. Serves 10.

Rebekah Leonard

My mother, Kris Abrahamsen Pedersen, often makes this using a venison roast. It is fantastic!

BARBECUED BEEF

2 lbs ground beef   4 Tbsp sugar
1 onion, diced   ½ cup water
2 Tbsp bacon drippings   1 tsp salt
1 14 oz. bottle catsup   ¼ tsp pepper
1 Tbsp prepared mustard   ¼ tsp paprika
1 Tbsp vinegar

Empty bottle of catsup into a saucepan and add mustard, vinegar, sugar, water, paprika, salt and pepper. Mix and place over low heat. Cover and simmer for 15 minutes. In a skillet combine bacon drippings with onion and cook over low hear until onions are transparent. Add ground beef and pepper to taste. Brown slowly, crumbling with a fork. When browned pour off excess grease, add barbecue sauce and cover. Simmer 15 minutes. Serve in hamburger buns.

Joyce Stedner

* * * * *

On the subject of spinach: divide into little piles. Rearrange again into new piles. After five or six maneuvers, sit back and say you are full.
Delia Ephron, How To Eat Like A Child

BARBECUED SPARERIBS

3-4 lb ribs, cut into serving
   sizes pieces
1 lemon
1 large onion
1 cup catsup

1/3 cup Worcestershire sauce
2 dashes Tabasco sauce
1 tsp chili powder
1 tsp salt
2 cups water

Preheat oven 450°F. Place ribs in a shallow roasting pan, meaty side up. On each piece, place a slice of lemon and onion. Roast for 20 minutes. Combine remaining ingredients, bring to a boil and pour over ribs after roasting. Continue baking in moderate oven 350°F until tender, 45 minutes to 1 hour. Baste ribs every 15 minutes. If sauce gets too thick, add water.

JoAnne Lindsley

Long time Lindsley family favorite- lemon is the secret ingredient.

HAM AND POTATO SKILLET

1 1lb ham slice
1 Tbsp oleo
1 Tbsp brown sugar
1 can cream of mushroom
   soup
2/3 cup milk
1/3 cup water

1/4 cup onions, cut up
1/2 tsp salt (optional)
1/8 tsp pepper
3 cups raw potatoes, sliced
   and peeled
1 cup raw carrots, sliced

In a 10 inch skillet, brown ham slice in oleo and brown sugar. Remove ham and pour off grease. Mix in same skillet: mushroom soup, milk, water, onions, salt and pepper. Stir in potatoes and carrots. Cover and cook over low heat, stirring now and then for about 35 minutes. Place ham on vegetables, cover and cook 10 more minutes. Serves 4.

Joyce Stedner

SEAFARER'S DINNER

2 cups (2 medium) sliced
   potatoes
1 cup (2 medium) carrots
1 medium onion, sliced and
   diced
16 oz. perch filets

½ tsp each dill weed and salt
⅛ tsp pepper
¼ cup margarine
¼ cup grated parmesan
   cheese
¼ tsp paprika

Heat oven to 425°F. In 1 ½ quart covered casserole layer potatoes, carrots, onion and perch. Sprinkle with ¼ tsp dill, ¼ tsp salt and ¹⁄₁₆ tsp pepper. Add 2 Tbsp margarine. Repeat layers. Cover and bake for 35-40 minutes. Remove cover and sprinkle with cheese and paprika. Continue baking for 10 minutes. Serves 4.

Anonymous

* * * * *

Consideration for others can mean taking a wing instead of a drumstick.

Garth Henrichs

COD WITH MUSHROOMS

4 Tbsp Butter - unsalted
4 Cloves Garlic
10 oz mushrooms - white
½ Cup Vermouth - dry
3 ½ Tbsp Parsley

1 Tbsp Balsamic Vinegar
½ tsp Kosher Salt
¼ tsp Black pepper, ground
4 Skinless Cod Fillets

In a heavy 12-inch skillet, melt 3 Tbsp. of the butter over medium-high heat. Add the mushrooms and cook, stirring only occasionally, until well browned, 5 to 7 minutes. Add the garlic and cook, stirring, until golden and fragrant, about 45 seconds. Add the vermouth, 3 Tbsp. of the parsley, the vinegar, salt, and pepper and boil until the liquid is reduced by half, about 2 minutes. Remove the pan from the heat, lightly season the cod with salt and pepper and add it to the pan (tuck under the tails if necessary to even out the thickness), nestling the fillets into the mushrooms and spooning some of the mushrooms on top. Bring the mixture to a gentle simmer over medium heat, cover the pan, reduce to medium low, and simmer until just cooked through (use the tip of a paring knife to check), 7 to 12 minutes, depending on thickness. With a slotted spatula, transfer the fish to serving plates or a platter.

Over low heat, whisk the remaining 1 Tbsp. butter into the sauce. Spoon the sauce over the fish and serve sprinkled with the remaining parsley. Yield: 4 servings.

Jim McKenney

The recipe works well with many types of fish. Mahi mahi, pollock, haddock, sole, flounder, sea bass, or halibut make perfect substitutes; reduce cooking time for thinner fillets.

* * * * *

Never eat more than you can lift.
Miss Piggy

STRIPED BASS WITH TOMATOES AND MUSHROOMS

6 Tbsp butter
¼ cup chopped onions
1 cup chopped mushrooms
1 tomato, peeled, seeded, and chopped
1 tsp. chopped chives
1 Tbsp chopped parsley
¾ cup fresh bread crumbs

salt
freshly ground black pepper to taste
1 three pound striped bass
1 Tbsp lemon juice
½ cup dry white wine
a little water

1. Preheat oven to 400°F.
2. In a skillet heat half the butter, add the onion and cook until it is transparent. Add the mushrooms and cook until wilted. Add the tomato and simmer for five minutes. Add the chives, parsley, bread crumbs, salt and pepper mix.
3. Stuff the fish loosely with the mixture and close the opening with skewers and string.
4. Place the fish in a baking pan lined with foil and sprinkle with the lemon juice, wine, and additional salt and pepper. Dot with the remaining butter and bake, uncovered, basting occasionally, until the fish flakes easily when tested with a fork, about thirty or forty minutes. Sprinkle with additional butter and lemon juice.

Mirella Affron

SALMON CAKES

½ lb salmon
1 egg
1 ½ cup matzoh meal
¼ cup milk

¼ tsp ground black pepper
¼ tsp garlic powder
vegetable oil

Poach the salmon until it is cooked thoroughly. Crumble it into small pieces. In a medium-sized bowl, mix all the ingredients except the oil. Form small patties. Fry the patties in the vegetable oil, turning occasionally, until the patties are golden brown.

Suggested accompaniment: Serve with a dip made by mixing ½ cup sour cream with 2 Tbsp ground horseradish.

Della Lee Sue

LACQUERED SALMON

1 C lite soy sauce
½ C orange juice
2 T cornstarch
1 T fresh ginger grated
1 T garlic crushed

½ C sliced scallions
2 T sherry
2 T honey
¼ t crushed red pepper
6 to 8 Salmon filets, skinless

Mix all of the ingredients except the salmon. Reserve ½ C of the liquid. Marinate the salmon in the liquid for an hour. Pre heat the broiler. Broil the salmon for 5 minutes on each side. Bring the reserved liquid to a boil to thicken and serve on the side. The marinade can be used with chicken, beef, vegetables or tofu.

Lee Ann Leichtfuss

* * * * *

Cauliflower is nothing but cabbage with a college education.

Mark Twain

SALMON WITH BEURRE ROUGE WITH SWEET PINK PEPPERCORNS

4 salmon filets seasoned
  with salt and pepper
½ cup of red wine
2 diced shallots
4 peppercorns
1 bay leaf

½ cup of heavy cream
¼ stick softened and cubed
  sweet butter
1 teaspoon dry pink
  peppercorns

Prepare the sauce first hold while cooking the fish
Preheat broiler or grill.

Grill or broil salmon 5 minutes on each side top with sauce and serve.

To prepare the sauce: Combine ½ cup of red wine, 2 diced shallots, 4 peppercorns and 1 bay leaf in a saucepot over medium heat and reduce until the wine is almost completely evaporated, stirring frequently.

Add ½ cup of heavy cream and reduce over medium high heat until almost evaporated, stirring frequently so that the cream doesn't burn. Transfer mixture to a double boiler and whisk in ¼ stick softened and cubed sweet butter, a little at a time, letting butter totally incorporate before adding more.

Strain sauce through a fine china cap or sieve. Add 1 teaspoon dry pink peppercorns and stir. Hold sauce in a warm area until ready for use.

Sandy Ingber

Sandy Ingber is Chef of the Oyster Bar in Grand Central Station NYC

* * * * *

A house is not beautiful because of its walls, but because of its cakes.

Old Russian Proverb

DOC'S RX FOR BAKED CLAMS

30 little neck clams on half
  shell
¾ Tbsp fresh lemon juice
¼ cup grated cheese
¼ cup seasoned bread
  crumbs

¼ cup finely chopped
  parsley
2 or 3 cloves garlic; crushed
1 tsp oregano
½ tsp salt
freshly ground pepper
olive oil

Preheat oven to 425°F. Loosen the meat in shells; drain well. Arrange clams (in their shells) in a shallow baking pan. Sprinkle each one with a little lemon juice. Combine the cheese, bread crumbs, parsley, garlic, oregano, salt and pepper and spoon the mixture over the clams. Put enough on each to cover the clam entirely, about 1 tsp per clam. Put about an eye dropper worth of oil on top of each one and bake 15 minutes. Serve with additional slices of lemon. Enjoy!

Ben Colucci, M. D.

ASIAN MUSSEL PASTA

2 lb PEI mussels, scrubbed,
  rinsed and dried
½ cup white wine
1 pint cherry tomatoes,
  halved
1 lb Blanched bucatelli, al
  dente

¾ cup Asian Tapenade, see
  recipe
¼ Thai or regular basil, cut
  into chiffonade
Kosher salt and freshly
  ground black pepper
Canola oil for cooking

In a wok or sauté pan, coated lightly with oil over medium heat, add mussels and stir fry for 15 seconds.

-Add wine and cover, cook until mussels start opening, about 3 minutes.

-Add tomatoes, pasta and Asian tapenade, toss well to combine and heat through and check for flavor.

-Toss with basil and serve

Sandy Ingber

Sandy Ingber is Chef of the Oyster Bar in Grand Central Station NYC

SUMPTUOUS SCALLOPS OVER LINGUINI

4 cloves of garlic.
½ c of extra virgin olive oil
Fresh chopped basil
4 medium sized plum
   tomatoes
¼ c chopped Spanish onion,
   (the taste of the scallops
   should dominate)

½ lb (8) large fresh bay
   scallops (4 serves two)
Fresh parsley
½ of a ¼ lb of butter.
½ lb of linguine, or home
   made even better.
Pinch or two of salt.
Smattering of fresh ground
   pepper.

Heat a deep frying pan on medium, then add a ¼ cup of olive oil. When oil is heated add chopped cloves of garlic. Add chopped onion. When garlic is slightly brown and onions soft, add chopped plum tomatoes slowly mixing them into the olive oil, garlic and onion mixture. Cook until the tomatoes are soft. Add several pinches of the chopped parsley. Add pepper to taste.

In meantime, bring slightly salted water in large sauce pan to low boil, I prefer to add a dollop or two of olive oil to the water.

Timing is important, when the linguine is added to the boiling water and is almost al dente -- cook the scallops by placing them on top of the tomato sauce mix. Keep turning the scallops, until they are white and soft.

Place a pat of butter over each scallop. When linguine is ready, drain in colander, replace in pan and add ½ stick of butter and mix. Mix in a little more olive oil. Salt to taste. Keep watching the scallops! With tongs place linguine in each of two deep dish plates. Add just a smidgen of pepper over each serving Put tomato sauce with each of the four scallops over the linguine. Sprinkle a pinch or two of parsley atop each scallop. Place a basil leave next to each scallops near rim of the dish for a gourmet touch.

John Hart

Serve with Chilled Italian Pinot Grigio.

SHRIMP & SCALLOP FRAICHE

½ c Creme Fraiche, recipe
  follows
1 c heavy cream
2 Tbsp sour cream
1 lb shrimp, cleaned, peeled
  and deveined
1 lb fresh sea scallops
salt & pepper to taste

½ stick butter
juice of 1 lemon
3 cloves of garlic, minced
1 Tbsp cognac or wine
1 Tbsp cornstarch
2 Tbsp fish or chicken stock
4 sprigs fresh parsley

For Creme Fraiche: Combine 1 c heavy cream & 2 Tbsp sour cream then cover with plastic wrap and let stand at room temperature for 12 to 24 hours. Salt & pepper shrimp and scallops (pat dry with paper towel).

Melt butter in a large skillet add lemon juice, Add shrimp and scallops and saute until scallops are opaque - 3 to 4 minutes per side. Remove to a warm platter. Add cognac or wine to pan juice.

Dissolve cornstarch in stock and add along with Creme Fraiche to pan and simmer until thickened. Pour sauce over shellfish and garnish with parsley.

Jeane Noud

Delicious over angel hair pasta.

SHRIMP SCAMPI

2 lbs large raw shrimp
¼ cup butter
1 tsp salt
6 cloves garlic, crushed

¼ cup chopped Italian
  parsley
2 tsp grated lemon peel
2 tsp lemon juice
6 lemon wedges

Preheat oven to 400°F. Remove shells from shrimp leaving shell on tail section only. Devein, wash under running water and drain. Melt butter in 13 x 9 baking dish. Add salt, garlic and 1 tbsp parsley; mix well. Arrange shrimp in a single layer in baking dish and bake, uncovered 5 minutes. Turn shrimp. Sprinkle with lemon peel, lemon juice and remaining parsley. Bake 8-9 minutes or just until tender. Arrange shrimp on heated serving platter. Pour garlic butter over all. Garnish with lemon wedges. Makes 6-8 servings.

Lois Colucci

SEAFOOD RISOTTO

½ onion chopped fine
1 T butter
1 t saffron
4 C chicken stock
1 C Arborio Rice

1 LB Shrimp
½ LB scallops
½ C parmesan
2 T chopped parsley

Bring the chicken sock to a boil add the saffron and reduce heat to low, just to keep it warm. Sauté the onion until transparent. Add the rice and sauté for one minute stirring constantly. Add the chicken stock a ½ cup at a time stirring constantly until one cup of the chicken stock is left. Add it all at one time with the shrimp and scallops stirring constantly until the seafood is finished, about 5 minutes. Add the parmesan and parsley and serve.

Lee Ann Leichtfuss

LINGUINI WITH WHITE CLAM SAUCE

24 cherrystone clams
⅓ cup olive oil
2 cloves garlic, crushed
¼ cup parsley, chopped

¼ tsp crushed red pepper
 (optional)
pinch of basil
salt and pepper

Open clams, reserve clam juice. Strain juice through a cheesecloth. Dice clams coarsely. In a small saucepan saute garlic for about 1 minute. Add clams, clam juice, parsley, red pepper, basil, salt and pepper to taste. Heat thoroughly and toss at once with linguini. (Linguini should be cooked while preparing the sauce.)

Ben Colucci, M. D.

* * * * *

Next to jazzy music, there is nothing that lifts the spirit and strengthens the soul more than a good bowl of chili.
Harry James

PENNE A LA VODKA

1 lb. penne
5 oz. butter
⅔ SKYY Vodka (or other midrange vodka)
¼ tsp red pepper flakes (or to your taste)

small can crushed plum tomatoes
¾ cup heavy cream
⅔ cup grated parmesan
1 pkg. frozen peas

Cook pasta, drain. Melt butter in large saucepan. Add vodka. Bring to a simmer for 2 minutes. Add crushed tomatoes and heavy cream. Return to simmer for 5 minutes. Remove from heat. Add pasta to sauce. Slowly mix in parmesan cheese. Add defrosted peas. Top with more parmesan cheese if desired.

Hints:

Serve with garlic bread.
May leave out peas, or replace with chicken.

Lauren Kreiger

KATHLEEN'S SPINACH LASAGNA

4 16 oz. cans crushed or plum tomatoes
2 boxes lasagna noodles (can used pre-boiled)
4 bags pre-washed spinach, remove stems!
2 packages whole milk mozzarella

4 2 lb. whole milk ricotta
2 bay leaves
7 cloves garlic
1 onion
oregano
olive oil
Optional: 2 beef bouillon cube

Preheat oven 325°F-350°F. Put olive oil in bottom of baking pan to prevent sticking.

Make 4 layers as follows:

one ladle tomato sauce
one layer noodles
one layer spinach
one layer mozzarella
Repeat 4 times.
Bake 1-1 ½ hours. For 10-12 hungry people. Enjoy!

Kathleen Muldoon
Ruth DeTar

BAKED MACARONI WITH ITALIAN SAUSAGE & PEPPERS

1 box whole wheat pasta
3 Tbsp olive oil
2 cloves of garlic-minced
1 Tbsp dried basil
4 c red spaghetti sauce
1 lb Italian sausage cooked
  & sliced thin

2 c shredded mozzarella,
  divided in half
1 c grated Parmesan cheese,
  divided in half
1 med onion, diced
2 green bell peppers, diced
2 red bell peppers, diced

Cook pasta according to pkg directions. Preheat oven to 350. Heat olive oil in large skillet and add garlic, onion, peppers and basil, saute 3 minutes, add sauce and sliced sausage, simmer 5 min.

Spread 1 c of sauce mixture on bottom of 13" x 9" baking dish. Layer ½ the macaroni, ½ the sauce mix, 1 c mozzarella and ½ c Parmesan and repeat. Bake 25 minutes. Let stand 10 min. before serving.

Jeane Noud

* * * * *

Any fool can count the seeds in an apple. Only God can count all the apples in one seed.

Robert Schuller

70208   **MAIN DISHES**   **63**

STUFFED PEPPERS

3 peppers (the more colorful, the better)
6 scallions
1 14 oz. container extra firm tofu
2 cups marinara sauce
½ cup basmati rice
½ cup quinoa

¼ cup walnuts (or nut of your choice)
1 tsp grated ginger
grated cheese
olive oil
salt, pepper, oregano and basil to taste

Prepare peppers by cutting them in half and cleaning the seeds out. Cover bottom half of a baking dish with water and olive oil. Place peppers cut side down in baking dish. Roast in oven at 375°F for 25 minutes (or until easily punctured with a knife). Turn peppers right side up and let cool in same dish. Prepare stuffing mixture by mixing rice and quinoa in 2 cups of water and cook covered for 30 minutes or until tender (or use a rice cooker). In a bowl mix together cooked grains, chopped walnuts, tofu (mashed or cut into small cubes- I prefer cubes), salt, pepper, chopped oregano, basil and 1 tsp of grated ginger. Grate cheese of choice (I've used several kinds: feta, cheddar, parmesan, Asiago, etc. about ¼ cup). In baking dish stuff peppers generously with mixture. Top with marinara sauce or sliced tomatoes. Sprinkle lightly with grated cheese and scallions on top. Cover bottom of baking dish with water. Start baking at 475°F for 10 minutes. Lower to 375°F for 10 minutes. Let sit in oven for 10 minutes before eating.

Food tip: This recipe is a twist on the familiar-improvising nurtures the seeds of discovery.... mmmmm

* * * * *

An apple is an excellent thing - until you have tried a peach.

George du Maurier

LISA'S MOTHER'S INDIAN PILAF

1¾ c. rice
3 c. chicken stock
1 tsp. curry powder
4 onions, sliced
½ c. white raisins
½ tsp. cinnamon
½ c. chopped almonds

2 small bay leaves
½ tsp. nutmeg
salt, pepper to taste
2 c. cooked turkey, chicken
  or lamb, cut in julienne
  strips

1. Cook rice in chicken stock and curry powder, 20 minutes.
2. In large pot, saute sliced onions till golden. Add raisins, cinnamon, almonds, bay leaves, nutmeg, pepper and salt. Mix. Add cooked rice and mix, Add cooked meat and mix thoroughly.
3. Put into casserole and refrigerate or freeze. When ready to serve, reheat, covered at 350 for 1 hour.

Mary Kroul McAlpin

This is a wonderful way to use leftover meats. Perfect for post-Thanksgiving when the turkey sandwich makings are looking kind of washed out. Also turns cold lamb into a treat.

WINTER CASSEROLE

4 cups squash, cooked and
  mashed (acorn or hubbard)
1 cup onion, chopped
1 ½ cups red and green
  peppers, chopped
3 cloves garlic, crushed
1 tsp ground cumin
4 eggs, beaten

½ tsp chili powder
½ tsp ground coriander
cayenne to taste
pepper to taste
salt to taste
olive oil to taste
1 cup grated cheese

Saute the onions, garlic and spices; when translucent add peppers. Cover and cook 8 minutes. Combine saute and squash, corn and eggs. Add seasonings as desired. Butter sides of casserole (2 quart size) and top with grated cheese. Bake at 350°F for 20 minutes covered and 15 minutes uncovered.

Tom Gale

SAUTEED CHARD AND COLLARDS WITH WHITE BEANS

Amounts are approximate- you can adjust in any way. You can also use only one type of green, or even more!

1 can white beans (navy or cannelloni)
olive oil (our daughter Ali who now lives in the almost South- Baltimore, says that it is best with bacon fat)
1 onion diced (you can ask for local Orange County onions at your grocery store all year round)

2-4 cloves garlic, chopped (garlic lovers can use even more)
1 bunch Swiss chard
1 bunch collards
1 jalapeno, minced (optional)
salt and pepper to taste

Lightly saute diced onion in oil (or bacon fat) until translucent. Clean greens and remove stems. Chop chard and collard stems and add them to the cooking onions. Coarsely chop greens and add with chopped garlic and diced jalapeno. Season with salt, and lots of fresh black pepper. Add 1-2 Tbsp water if needed, stir, cover and cook until greens reduce. Add White beans until heated through and serve over rice or pasta.

Variations:

- Add chopped hot or sweet Italian sausage (uncooked add in with the onions; or use leftover and add later to reheat)
- Add baby shrimp and season with cilantro
- Freeze in quart bags and add to chicken soup in the winter

Liana Hoodes
Dave Church

* * * * *

She did not so much cook as assassinate food.
Storm Jameson

MICHAEL'S TORTA FESTIVA
(Colorful Quiche)

2-3 large onions
1 red pepper
1 green pepper
1 gold pepper
1 large head garlic
1 12 oz. pkg. mushrooms
1 cup ricotta
8 oz. grated sharp cheddar

1 lb country sausage
  (optional)
5 eggs
1 Tbsp sage
¼ cup pine nuts
basil and/or oregano to taste
salt and pepper
garnish with sesame seeds

Saute onions and peppers in olive oil and spice with sage, salt and pepper. Set aside. In 2 Tbsp butter and 2 Tbsp olive oil saute garlic and add mushrooms. Saute for 2-5 minutes. Add to onion and peppers mixture. Saute 1 lb country sausage until cooked and add to veggies. Brown ¼ cup pine nuts in same pan as sausage. Add grated cheese and ricotta to veggies and sausage and mix. Beat eggs and mix in a bowl with all the ingredients. Pour into pie crusts or pie pans lined with whole wheat wrap. Bake at 375°F for 50 minutes. Yield 3 pies.

Michael Kanakis

POPOVER PIE

1 cup milk
2 eggs
½ tsp salt

1 cup flour
dash Tabasco
1 cup shredded cheese

Preheat oven to 350°F. Grease a 9 inch pie pan. Beat eggs and milk. Add flour, salt, and Tabasco to heavy cream consistency. Stir in cheese, pour into pie pan and bake 35 minutes. Pie will form a huge golden bubble that will settle down to a quiche, delicious hot or cold. Serves 6 to 8.

Variations: Add mushrooms, tuna, crabmeat, shrimp, bacon bits, ham, olives or any combination of these.

Lydia Stenzel

YOUR FAVORITE RECIPES

Recipe   Page Number

SIDE DISHES

Blue flag Iris
Austa Densmore Sturdevant (1855-1936)

Recipe Favorites

Page No.

Recipe Title:_____ _____

_____ _____

_____ _____

_____ _____

_____ _____

_____ _____

_____ _____

_____ _____

_____ _____

_____ _____

Family Favorites

Page No.

Recipe Title:_____ _____

_____ _____

_____ _____

_____ _____

_____ _____

Notes:_____

_____

_____

_____

SIDE DISHES

MARINATED ASPARAGUS

1 lb asparagus
¼ cup soy sauce
½ teaspoon sugar
½ teaspoon cider vinegar

2 teaspoons sesame oil (can
substitute olive, canola,
etc.)
Chopped garlic (optional to
your taste)

Cut ends of asparagus. Boil water and cook for 1 minute, rinse in cold water.

Combine above ingredients and marinate overnight. Rotate as often as possible.

Jeanne Capobianco

I do not boil mine. They tend to soften enough through the marination process. I use a lot of fresh chopped garlic. The thinner the stalks, the better this works.)

CHINESE BEANS

1 Tbsp. Soy
1 Tbsp. Honey
1 Tbsp. Butter

2 Tbsp. Olive Oil
Kosher Salt
Minced Garlic

Combine Soy & Honey in small bowl. Heat Butter, & Olive Oil in 10 Skillet. When Butter melts add Beans I Pinch Kosher Salt cook 'til tender and brown approx 7-8 min. Reduce heat to low, add garlic stir 20 sec. Add soy mixture stir til coated. Reduce liquid 45 sec.

Jim McKenney

* * * * *

Life expectancy would grow by leaps and bounds if green vegetables smelled as good as bacon.

Doug Larson

BAKED TOMATOES WITH HERBS

4 large tomatoes
¼ cup butter/margarine
  melted
1 clove garlic, mashed
few leaves basil, chopped
  fine
½ tsp thyme

salt to taste
4-5 slices bread, cut into ½
  cubes (sourdough or other
  firm bread is best)
½ cup Parmesan cheese (or
  more, to taste)

Remove centers of tomatoes and save pulp. Place tomatoes in shallow greased 4-quart baking dish. Mix butter, garlic, basil, thyme, salt and bread. Add tomato pulp and mix gently. Stuff tomatoes with mixture. Sprinkle with Parmesan cheese. Bake at 350°F for 30 minutes.

Anonymous

EGGPLANT

eggplant   corn meal

In Georgia, where I spent much of my childhood, cooking with a "streak of lean, streak of fat" was basic. Greasy vegetables - the best. No More. Here is a healthy way to cook eggplant which is known for its affinity for oil.

Peel and slice crosswise ⅛-¼ inch thick. Sprinkle with salt as you layer slices into bowl. Leave several hours to "weep". (A weight on top hastens the process) Drain, dip slices on both sides in yellow or white corn meal. Put in Griswold (cast iron) pan with a little olive oil, and as pan begins to smoke, brown on both sides, then cover and cook slowly until done through (taste). Garlic flakes enhance eggplant. Left over slices are great with tomato, onion, cheese, baked in a shallow dish. The crunchy cornbread exterior is a nice contrast to the soft eggplant. Actually, good for squash and other vegetables.

Mary E. Thurston

Full disclosure: I use bacon grease - more flavor!

CURRIED CARROTS & LENTILS

½ C dried red lentils
1 ½ C water
3 carrots, peeled and cut
   into ½" pieces
½ C chopped onions

¼ C golden raisins
2 Tbsp unsalted butter
1 tsp salt
½ tsp fennel seeds

Combine lentils and ½ C water in 2 qt. microwave safe casserole. Cover, cook full power 5 minutes. (If water foams and spills over, replace with 1-2 Tbsp water.) Stir in carrots and ½ C water. Cover and cook 5 minutes. Stir in remaining ½ C water and all other ingredients. Cover, cook 5 minutes. 4-6 servings.

Ruth Diem

CURRIED LENTILS

1 c. lentils
2 onions, chopped
4 T. oil
2-3 cloves garlic, minced
2 c. stock or water

3 Tbsp. curry powder
2 T. turmeric
salt to taste
freshly ground pepper to
   taste

1. Saute onions and garlic in oil for 5-10 minutes until soft.
2. Add lentils, stock, curry powder, turmeric, salt and pepper. Bring to rolling boil, cover and turn off heat. Let rest 1 hour.
3. After 1 hour check level of liquid and simmer until lentils are cooked, 2-2 ½ hours. Add water if necessary.
4. Serve hot or cold. If serving cold accompany with yogurt and/or chopped raw onions. Serves 4.

Mary Kroul McAlpin

Wonderfully versatile, it can be an appetizer, a vegetarian main dish or a side dish.

* * * * *

The New York Times has described the bagel as "an unsweetened doughnut with rigor mortis."

MIDDLE EAST CARROT SALAD

2 cup coarsely chopped
  carrot
1 cup uncooked large round
  couscous (or orzo)
2 ¼ cups water
3 tbsp chopped cilantro
¼ tsp lemon zest

1 tbsp lemon juice
½ tsp round cumin
1 cinnamon stick
2 tbsp chopped parsley
2 ½ tbsp olive oil
¾ tsp salt
1 clove garlic, minced

Combine carrots, couscous, water and cinnamon stick in a saucepan. Bring to a boil and cook 10 minutes or until tender. Cool and drain. Combine with cilantro, and remaining ingredients. Toss gently to coat. Yields 8 servings.

Mary Davidson

LIME HORSERADISH JELLO SALAD

2 pkg. lime Jello
3 c. boiling water
2 c. cottage cheese
1 c. mayonnaise

½ pint heavy cream
4 Tbsp. horseradish, or more
  to taste
juice of 2 lemons

1. Mix Jello with boiling water and chill until it has consistency of egg whites.
2. Mix cottage cheese to loosen, blend in mayonnaise, horseradish and lemon juice.
3. Whip cream and fold into cottage cheese mixture.
4. Fold all into Jello, pour into serving dish and allow to set.

Mary Kroul McAlpin

Completely out of fashion, but it's so incredibly good I couldn't leave it out. Tune in to "A Prairie Home Companion" as you make it. Perfect with ham.

* * * * *

Food, glorious food!
Oliver Twist

MARTHA'S ARKANSAS CORN BREAD SALAD

Arkansas Corn Bread:

1 heaping c. corn meal
  (white is authentic)
4 tsp. baking powder
1 tsp. salt (scant)
⅛ tsp. soda

1 rounded Tbsp. flour
1 egg
1 c. buttermilk or yogurt
2 Tbsp. butter

1. Oven at 450°F.
2. Combine corn meal, baking powder, soda and salt.
3. Meanwhile, place butter in 8x10 inch baking pan and put in oven.
4. Combine egg and buttermilk or yogurt and mix well. Add to dry ingredients and stir just enough to combine.
5. Immediately pour into hot pan and bake 20 minutes, or until well browned.
   6. Run metal spatula under corn bread to loosen and turn onto platter. Let cool.

Corn Bread Salad:

1 pan Arkansas corn bread
2 c. mayonnaise, or to taste
1 bunch scallions or 1 onion,
  chopped
3 medium tomatoes, coarsely
  chopped
1 green pepper, coarsely
  chopped

4 stalks celery, chopped
1 16 oz. can whole kernel
  corn, Niblets or drained, or
  equivalent in leftover
  corn-on-the-cob, cut off the
  cob

1. Tear corn bread into smallish pieces and place in mixing bowl.
2. Add vegetables and mayonnaise.
3. Toss lightly to combine.

Mary Kroul McAlpin

For best results use the recipe for dense Arkansas corn bread

CARAMELIZED ONIONS AND MASHED POTATOES

8 potatoes, whatever you
  have but russet is great
2-3 large onions, Vidalia are
  best

1 stick butter
salt and pepper to taste
⅔ cup whole milk or cream

Peel and boil potatoes (potatoes should be put into cold water then brought to a boil) until they are soft. Meanwhile thinly slice onions and add them to melted butter, saute onions until they are brown, but not burned or hard so use a low heat.

Mash potatoes with hand masher and add cream and salt and pepper to taste.

Angelena Abate

POTATOES CHANTILLY

6 large all-purpose potatoes,
  about 4 ½ lbs peeled and
  quartered
⅔ c milk
5 Tbsp butter or margarine

1 tsp salt
½ tsp pepper
1 c heavy cream
¾ c grated Cheddar cheese

Put potatoes in enough water for them to boil, then reduce heat and cook until tender, 12-15 minutes. Preheat oven to 350°F. Butter a 3 qt baking dish. Drain potatoes, set aside. In the same pot warm milk over low heat. When warm, remove from heat add potatoes, butter, salt, and pepper. Beat mixture until smooth. Spread mashed potatoes in the baking dish. Beat the heavy cream until soft peaks form and spread on potatoes. Sprinkle with cheese. Bake until the cheese melts and the top is golden brown - about 45 minutes.

Jeane Noud

* * * * *

Forget love... I'd rather fall in chocolate!
Unknown

COMPANY POTATOES

4-6 c. cooked, cubed potatoes
¼ c. chopped green pepper
¼ c. chopped onion
¼ c. chopped pimento
(optional)
2 Tbsp. fresh parsley
¼ lb. yellow American
cheese, diced (you can use
Velveeta cheese)

½ c butter
½ c milk
½ c crushed corn flake
crumbs
1 slice bread, cubed small
Salt and pepper to taste

Toss all the above carefully. Put in greased casserole. Cover and refrigerate.

When you are ready, melt ½ c butter and ½ c milk; pour over potatoes. Sprinkle with corn flake crumbs. Bake at 350°F for 35-40 minutes.

Marina Davis

* * * * *

Too many cooks may spoil the broth, but it only takes one to burn it.
Madeleine Bingham, The Bad Cook's Guide

SMASHED POTATOES

Dz. baby potatoes
Olive Oil
Kosher Salt

Gorgonzola Cheese
(optional)

Put a dozen or so baby potatoes in a pot of water with 2 tsp kosher salt, cook until completely tender and can be easily pierced with a fork (about 30-35 minutes).

Set up a double layer of clean dishtowels. Place each potatoes between the towels and gently press down on each potato to flatten it to a thickness of about ½ inch. Try not to break them. Cover a large rimmed baking sheet with aluminum foil and then parchment on top of that.

Transfer flattened potatoes carefully to prepared baking sheet and let cool (Optional-completely at room temperature, or cover loosely with plastic wrap and refrigerate for up to 8 hours.)

In a hot oven, 450°F (or 400° convection), sprinkle the potatoes with kosher salt and pour extra virgin olive oil over them; optionally, add Gorgonzola cheese to the top of each potato.

Lift the potatoes gently to make sure some of the oil goes underneath them and they are well coated on both sides.

Roast the potatoes until they're crispy and deep brown around the edges, turning after about 15 minutes, for about 30 minutes total for convection oven (or closer to 40 minutes if roasting conventionally).

Jim McKenney

* * * * *

When baking, follow directions. When cooking, go by your own taste.

Laiko Bahrs

PARSNIP, CARROT AND LEEK GRATIN

2 Tbsp butter
2 lbs leeks (use only white
  and pale green parts)
  rinsed, halved lengthwise,
  cut crosswise into 10 inch
  pieces (about 5 cups)
1 ½ lbs large carrots, peeled,
  cut diagonally into ¼ inch
  slices

1 ½ lbs large parsnips,
  peeled, cut diagonally
  into ¼ inch slices
2 ½ cups whipping cream
2 Tbsp fresh sage, chopped
2 tsp Dijon mustard
¾ tsp salt
½ tsp pepper
½ cup coarsely grated
  Parmesan cheese

Preheat oven to 400°F. Butter/grease 9x13 inch baking dish. Melt 2 Tbsp butter in large, heavy skillet over medium low heat. Add leeks and saute until soft and beginning to color, 15 minutes or more (as much as 30 minutes if leeks are tough). Transfer to large bowl. Cook carrots and parsnips in large pots of boiling, salted water until almost tender, about 3 minutes or more. Drain well, place in bowl with leeks. Whisk cream, sage, mustard and pepper to blend in a medium bowl. Pour cream mixture over vegetables and stir gently to combine. Transfer to prepared baking dish. Sprinkle with Parmesan cheese. Cover dish with foil. Bake for 30 minutes. Uncover and bake until vegetables are tender, top is golden brown and cream is thickened, about 30 minutes more. Let stand 20 minutes. Serve hot.

Anonymous

Unbelieveably good. At a holiday buffet; better than dessert!

* * * * *

How can a nation be great if its bread tastes like Kleenex?

Julia Child

CAUCASIAN RICE

2 cups long grain rice
½ cup pine nuts or blanched
  almonds
½ cup finely chopped onions
¼ cup seedless raisins
4 cups chicken stock
  (canned is okay)
1 tsp salt

¼ tsp cinnamon
⅛ lb mushroom (or 1 small
  can)
⅓ tsp allspice
½ lb chicken giblets
  (optional)
ground black pepper

Wash rice thoroughly. Place in casserole and mix with the nuts, raisins, onions, mushrooms, giblets and seasonings. Have the chicken stock boiling and add it to mixture. Cover and bake in 350°F oven for 30 minutes. Mix well, recover and bake for another 15 minutes. Do not over cook. Remove lid and let stand in warm oven until ready to serve. Serves 6.

Liona K. Howell

RICE CASSEROLE

3 cups cooked rice
¼ cup sugar
1 egg, beaten

1 apple
½ cup raisins
1 tsp oil

Grease a loaf pan with 1 tsp oil. Core, peel and slice the apple. Set the apple aside. Mix the rice, sugar, egg and raisins in a mixing bowl. Put half the rice mixture into the loaf pan. Add apple slices. Cover the apples with the remaining rice mixture. Bake in the oven at 350°F for 30-35 minutes, or until golden brown. Serve hot. Makes 4-6 servings. This dish is a nice accompaniment to roast chicken.

Della Lee Sue

* * * * *

There is no love sincerer than the love of food.
George Bernard Shaw

CORN CASSEROLE

1 box Jiffy cornbread mix
2 beaten eggs
1 12-14 oz. can creamed corn
1 12-14 oz. can kernel corn
(drained)

1 8 oz. container of sour
cream
1 stick melted butter

Combine all ingredients and place into a greased 8x8 inch or 9x9 inch baking pan. Bake at 350°F for 40-60 minutes. It is delicious!

Paula Medley

BROCCOLI-PEA CASSEROLE

2 boxed pkg frozen chopped
broccoli
1 boxed pkg frozen peas,
thawed (run warm water
over them in a strainer)
1 can cream of mushroom
soup
1 cup mayonnaise

1 cup grated sharp cheddar
cheese
2 eggs beaten
1 medium onion, chopped
½ cup crushed round
crackers (Ritz)
salt and pepper to taste

Cook broccoli according to directions. Drain. Arrange ½ of broccoli in greased 2-quart casserole dish. Cover with layer of peas. Mix mushroom soup, mayonnaise, cheese, onions, eggs, salt and pepper to make a sauce. Pour ½ of sauce over broccoli and peas. Add rest of broccoli and top with remaining sauce. Sprinkle crushed crackers on top. Bake at 350°F for 30 minutes.

Anonymous

* * * * *

The first time I ate organic whole-grain bread I swear it tasted like roofing material.

Robin Williams

SPINACH PIE

1 pkg frozen chopped
spinach, thawed and well
drained

1 egg
2 ready made pie crusts
2 Tbsp parmesan cheese

Preheat oven to 350°F. Mix spinach, parmesan cheese and egg together. Pour into crust. Add second crust to top. Bake 30-40 minutes until golden.

April Marl
In memory of my Nana Rose.

Cover edges with foil to avoid over browning.

ZUCCHINI SQUARES

5 cups shredded zucchini (or
I guess it can be thinly
sliced)
1 ½ cups Bisquick
1 cup chopped onion
6 eggs beaten (or substitute
fake eggs, Southwestern or
vegetable)

1 cup shredded cheddar
cheese (or more to sprinkle
on top)
¾ cup vegetable oil
¾ tsp salt
2 cloves garlic, minced

Optional: Several good shakes of green pepper Tabasco sauce (not red, the green Tabasco is not hot; it's yummy), Mrs. Dash's original seasoning, some chopped red pepper, or whatever suits your fancy.

Lightly grease 9x13 inch pan. I just mix everything together and spread into the pan. At that point, I often sprinkle extra cheese on top and sometimes slice tomatoes on top for a nice presentation because it all bakes together and adds some color. Bake in a preheated oven at 350°F for 35-40 minutes or until a toothpick comes out clean or is a nice golden brown. Be sure to look in on it after about a half hour. Cool and cut into squares for serving. Can be easily microwaved.

Anonymous

These are great for a quick light lunch, a breakfast on the go, cut-up small for appetizers or as an accompaniment to just about any entree. I bumped up the original recipe (billed as an appetizer) to make a more formidable square.

BREAKFAST

Butter & Eggs
Austa Densmore Sturdevant (1855-1936)

Recipe Favorites

Page No.

Recipe Title:_____

_____
_____
_____
_____
_____
_____
_____
_____
_____

Family Favorites

Page No.

Recipe Title:_____

_____
_____
_____
_____
_____

Notes:_____

_____
_____
_____

BREAKFAST

DEVILED SCRAMBLED EGGS

6 eggs
½ c sour cream
1 tsp prepared mustard
½ tsp salt

¼ tsp pepper
2 tbs butter
paprika

Beat eggs slightly. Add sour cream mixed with mustard, salt, pepper. Heat butter in frying pan, pour in eggs and cook slowly until done. Sprinkle with paprika.

Mary

BREAKFAST CASSEROLE

8 slices bacon
2 onions thinly sliced
12 slices of buttered potato
   bread
½ lbs shredded Swiss cheese

8 large eggs
4 c milk or ½ & ½
1 ½ tsp salt
¼ tsp pepper

Cook the bacon and crumble. Beat the eggs, add milk and salt & pepper.

In an oven proof casserole layer buttered bread, bacon, onion, cover with eggs & milk mixture. Cover the top with cheese and bake at 350 for 45-50 minutes until eggs are set and top is brown.

Mary Ann Maurer

Omit the bacon for a vegetarian treat.

* * * * *

To eat well in England you should have breakfast three times a day.

W. Somerset Maugham

IMPOSSIBLE PIE
(Quiche)

12 slices bacon, crisply fried
  and crumbled
1 C shredded Swiss cheese
⅓ C chopped onion
2 C milk

1 C Bisquick
4 eggs
¼ t salt
⅛ t pepper

Heat oven to 400°F. Grease 10 inch pan. Sprinkle bacon, cheese, onion in pan. Beat remaining ingredients until smooth (15 seconds in blender on high or 1 minute with hand mixer). Bake until knife comes out clean, 35-40 minutes.

Anonymous

CORN FRITTERS

2 eggs
4 tsp Flour
¼ tsp Salt

2 ½ c Corn, Canned/Frozen
  or Fresh

1 cup corn & 1 egg = 5 fritters.
Separate eggs. Mix together well-beaten egg yolks, flour, salt & corn. Whip whites until stiff but not dry. Fold in corn mixture. Fry at med. heat until cooked.

Jim McKenney

Yield: 4 servings

SWEET PANCAKES

2 c flour
3 eggs
1 c milk
1 tsp salt
2 tbsp maple syrup

1 tbsp melted butter
1 tsp baking powder
butter or vegetable oil for
  skillet

Sift flour then slowly mix in the rest of the ingredients and beat until thoroughly mixed.
Put small amount of butter or oil in a skillet, heat (skillet is hot enough when a drop of water sizzles). I use a quarter cup measure to make pancakes. Cook until golden brown.

Anastasia Maurer Wagner

FINNISH OVEN PANCAKE

5 large eggs
1 Tbsp sugar
½ tsp salt
2 ½ cup milk

1 cup small curd cottage
  cheese
1 cup flour
1 tsp baking powder
½ cup butter, cut into pieces

Preheat oven to 425°F. Place 9x13 pan in oven to heat. In large bowl beat eggs, sugar, and salt until thick and about tripled in volume. Add milk, cottage cheese, flour, and baking powder; mix well. Add butter to hot pan and swirl it around to coat the bottom. Pour batter into pan. Bake until well browned and puffed high around the sides, about 25 minutes. Serve with lemon and powdered sugar.

Sarah Mack

* * * * *

My wife and I tried to breakfast together, but we had to stop or our marriage would have been wrecked.
Winston Churchill

OVERNIGHT FRENCH TOAST

1 loaf French bread (or
  Italian)
8 large eggs
2 cups ½ and ½
1 cup milk
2 Tbsp sugar

1 Tbsp vanilla
½ tsp cinnamon (optional)
½ tsp nutmeg (optional)
⅛ tsp salt
butter

Butter a 9x13 inch baking pan. Cut loaf of bread into 1 inch slices (should be about 20). Put slices in the pan in two rows. They should be sitting up slightly and overlap. Combine the eggs, milk, ½ and ½, vanilla, salt and spices (if desired) in a mixing bowl. Mix and pour over the bread slices. Make sure to get the mixture soaking into all the pieces of bread. Cover the pan and leave it overnight in the refrigerator. (My mom likes to put it out in the garage if the temperature is below 40°F because the pan takes up so much room in the fridge!)

In the morning, preheat the oven to 350°F. Make a Pecan Streusel topping while the oven is heating up. Mix 2 sticks of butter, 1 cup packed brown sugar, 1 cup chopped pecans, 2 Tbsp real maple syrup and an optional ½ tsp each of cinnamon and nutmeg together in a bowl. (We make the cinnamon and nutmeg optional because my mom doesn't like either one) When these ingredients are mixed together sprinkle them atop the slices of bread prepared earlier. Bake for 30-45 minutes, the bread should be a golden brown color.

**Rebekah Leonard, with help from mom,
Kristine Abrahamsen Pedersen**

This is our new family favorite for Christmas morning. It also reheats well for late night snacking. Use real maple syrup from local sugar houses for the yummiest results!

* * * * *

I am not a glutton I am an explorer of food.
Erma Bombeck

COFFEE CAKE

1 pint sour cream   2 tsp baking soda

Mix together and put in refrigerator while you make the batter.

Batter:

4 eggs   1 tsp vanilla
¼ lb margarine   2 tsp baking powder
2 c sugar   3 c sifted flour

Topping:

1 c sugar   1 sm box of raisins (⅓ c)
2 tsp cinnamon   chopped nuts (optional)

Mix all batter ingredients together and then add the sour cream mixture from the refrigerator and mix again.

Grease bottom and sides of the pan, pour in batter and sprinkle the topping on the top. Swirl with a knife like you would a marble cake. Make sure the raisins are covered with batter or they will get hard. Bake at 350°F for one hour or until done when tested

Jeane Noud

12 ½ inch round pan or 13x9x2 inch rectangular pan can be used.

BISQUICK COFFEE CAKE WITH STREUSEL TOPPING

Coffee Cake:

2 C Bisquick   ¾ C milk
1 T sugar   1 egg

Topping:

⅓ C brown sugar   ¼ C butter
⅓ C Bisquick   ½ t cinnamon

Mix cake ingredients together only until moist (do not overbeat). Mix topping ingredients together and pour on top of coffee cake. Bake at 400° for 20-25 minutes.

Ruth Diem

APRICOT/PRUNE COFFEECAKE

Streusel topping:

½ C brown sugar, packed
2 T flour

1 T cinnamon
2 T butter

Batter:

¾ C chopped dried apricots
3 C sifted flour
¼ t salt
¾ C butter or margarine
4 eggs
1 C sour cream

¾ C chopped dried prunes
1 ½ T baking powder
¾ t soda
1 ½ C sugar
1 ½ t vanilla
2 T confectioners' sugar

Mix streusel ingredients. Grease and flour 10 inch tube pan. On waxed paper sift 3 C flour, baking powder, baking soda and salt. Beat butter till fluffy and add sugar slowly, then eggs, one at a time. Beat 3 minutes till light and fluffy. Add vanilla. Divide flour in 4 parts and slowly beat in alternating with sour cream, starting and ending with flour. Beat just until smooth. Fold in prunes and apricots.

Turn ⅓ batter into Bundt pan, sprinkle with ½ streusel. Repeat layering. Bake at 350° for 55-60 minutes. Let cool in pan for 20 minutes. Remove carefully. Sift confectioners' sugar over top.

Ruth Diem

YUMMY COFFEE CAKE

½ C Butter
1 C Sugar
2 Eggs, beaten
1 teaspoon Vanilla

1 C sour cream
2 C flour, sifted w/1 or 2 tsp
    baking powder and 1 ¼ tsp
    baking soda

Topping Ingredients:

¼ C Brown Sugar
½ C Pecan nuts

1 tsp Cinnamon
1 tsp Nutmeg

Mix together.

Cream butter and sugar then add other ingredients one at a time including sour cream. Slowly mix all the flour into the mixture. When thoroughly mixed pour half the batter in tube pan alternate with half the topping. Bake 35-40 minutes at 350°F in a tube pan.

Mary Ann Maurer

NANTUCKET MORNING GLORY MUFFINS

2 ¼ C all-purpose flour
1 T ground cinnamon
2 T baking soda
½ t salt
1 ¼ C sugar
½ C shredded coconut
½ C raisins
2 C grated carrots (3-4
  loosely packed)

1 apple shredded
1 C canned crushed
  pineapple, drained
½ C chopped pecans or
  walnuts
3 large eggs
1 C vegetable oil
1 t vanilla extract

Preheat oven to 350°F. Grease a 12 cup muffin tin or line cups with foil baking cups.

Sift together the flour, cinnamon, baking soda and salt into a large bowl. Stir in the sugar. Add coconut, raisins, carrots, apple, pineapple and chopped nuts. Mix well.

In separate bowl whisk eggs with vegetable oil and vanilla, then pour into the bowl with the other ingredients. Stir well.

Fill each muffin cup to the brim. Bake for 35 minutes or until a toothpick inserted in the center of the muffin comes out clean. Cool the muffins in the pan for 10 minutes and turn out onto a rack to finish cooling.

Ruth Diem

* * * * *

We didn't starve, but we didn't eat chicken unless we were sick, or the chicken was.

Bernard Malamud

YOUR FAVORITE RECIPES

Recipe   Page Number

BREADS & PASTRIES

Lemon Day Lily
Austa Densmore Sturdevant (1855-1936)

Recipe Favorites

Page No.

Recipe Title:_____

_____ _____

_____ _____

_____ _____

_____ _____

_____ _____

_____ _____

_____ _____

_____ _____

_____ _____

Family Favorites

Page No.

Recipe Title:_____

_____ _____

_____ _____

_____ _____

_____ _____

_____ _____

Notes:_____

_____

_____

_____

702-08

BREADS & PASTRIES

WHITE BREAD

2 cups milk
2 Tbsp butter
1 tsp salt
2 Tbsp sugar

2 pkg dry yeast
¼ cup water (lukewarm!!)
6 cups flour

Heat ¼ cup water and butter until it starts to melt (not too hot!!). In a bowl add yeast and stir well. Add salt, sugar and milk. Mix. Start with 4 cups of flour. Kneed until flour doesn't stick to your fingers adding other 2 cups of flour as you go. Cover and let rise until it comes to the top of your bowl. Turn out onto a floured surface and kneed down. Cut into 3 loaves, or rolls. Let dough rise again in greased pans for about 45 minutes. Bake in a 345°F oven for 45 minutes.

Mrs. Clyde Marl (Mary)

Mrs. Marl has lived here in Cragsmoor for 76 years.

COUNTRY ITALIAN BREAD

2 cups warm water
   (110°-115°F)
¼ tsp sugar
1 ½ tsp active dry yeast

5 cups unbleached flour
1 Tbsp salt
2 Tbsp olive oil

In a bowl, combine water and sugar, sprinkle yeast over top. Let stand 10 minutes. In a mixing bowl, combine flour, salt and olive oil. Add dissolved yeast and mix with wooden spoon to form a soft dough. Knead by hand or machine until smooth and elastic. Put dough in a bowl greased with margarine. Cover and let rise in a warm place for 1 ½ hours. Punch down, rise again 1 hour. Punch down and divide dough in half. Roll each half into a loaf shape. Place in bread pans greased with margarine. Allow to rise for 1 hour. Bake in a 450°F oven for 15-20 minutes. Remove loaves from pans. Reduce heat to 350°F and continue baking for about 30 minutes or until loaves sound hollow when tapped. Makes 2 loaves of 18 inches (20 slices per loaf).

Marie (Freddie) Peterson

CHALLAH

1 Tbsp yeast	2 tsp salt
2 tsp sugar (or 1 ½ tsp honey)	2 eggs
	2 Tbsp salad oil
1 ¼ cups warm water	1 egg yolk
4 ½ cups sifted flour	poppy seeds

Combine yeast, sugar, and ½ cup water. Let stand for 10 minutes. Sift flour and salt into bowl and make a well in the center. Drop in eggs, oil, remaining water and yeast mixture. Work into flour. Knead on floured surface until smooth and elastic. Place in bowl and brush top with oil. Cover with towel and let rise in a warm place for 1 hour. Punch down and let rise until doubled in bulk. Brush with egg yolk and sprinkle with poppy seeds. Bake in preheated oven at 375°F for about 50 minutes or until brown. Makes 1 challah.

Ann Butter

BEER BREAD

3 c self rising flour	1 can of beer
3 tbs sugar	2 tbs melted butter
1 pinch of salt	

Mix all ingredients together except butter. Put finished dough into bread pan and bake at 350 for ½ hour. Remove from oven and spread butter on top of bread. Bake for additional ½ hour.

Dad Maurer

* * * * *

I never worry about diets. The only carrots that interest me are the number you get in a diamond.

Mae West

BUTTERHORN ROLLS

1 Pack Yeast
¼ Cup Water (warm 110°)
¾ Cup Milk, scalded
½ Cup Shortening

½ Cup Sugar
1 tsp Salt
3 ea Eggs
4 ½ Cu Flour, enriched-sift

Soften yeast in warm (110deg) ¼ cup water. Combine milk, shortening, sugar, & salt. Cool to lukewarm; Add yeast, mix well; Add eggs, then flour - mix smooth & knead. Place in greased bowl to rise until double in size. Divide into thirds, roll to 9" diameter and cut into 9-12 wedges. Let rise on greased pan. Bake at 400 for 7-8 min. until light brown. Yield: 12 servings

Jim McKenney

IRISH SODA BREAD

4 C sifted flour
1 T sugar
1 t salt
1 ½ t baking soda
1 t baking powder

1 ¾ C buttermilk
1 C raisins
2 T caraway seeds
2 T melted butter

Heat oven to 350°. Sift flour, sugar, salt and baking soda and powder. Add buttermilk. Stir till all dry ingredients are moistened. Stir in raisins and caraway seeds. Turn dough out onto floured board. Knead 10 times. Form ball, place on greased cookie sheet. Bake 50-60 minutes. Brush with melted butter.

Ruth Diem

LUCY'S SPOONBREAD

1 cup cornmeal
1 cup boiling water
1 cup milk

1 egg
4 Tbsp butter
1 ½ tsp baking powder

Pour boiling water over cornmeal and let sit for 5 minutes. Mix rest of ingredients into cornmeal. Pour into buttered baking dish and bake for 40 minutes at 375°F.

Lucy Muller

Delicious with chili or by itself with butter.

MEXICAN CORN BREAD

¼ C vegetable oil
1 medium onion, chopped
1 garlic clove, minced
1 red bell pepper, finely
  chopped
1 can creamed corn

1 ½ c self rising corn meal
¾ c grated Monterey Jack or
  Cheddar cheese
2 lge eggs
1 c buttermilk

Heat 2 tbs of the oil in a cast iron skillet. Mix together all ingredients including the rest of the oil. When it gets hot, pour the mixture in the oiled skillet and bake at 400 degrees for 30 minutes or until browned.

Jeane Noud

Let it sit for a couple of minutes and check to see if it is done before cutting

TOMATO BREAD

8 oz. canned chopped
  tomatoes, reserve 1 or 2 oz
  liquid to adjust
  consistency. (the new
  seasoned ones are good) or
  you use an 8 oz jar of
  salsa)
2 to 2 ¼ c flour

1 ½ t yeast
½ t salt
½ t sugar
½ t Italian seasoning
2 t butter
½ t ground black pepper
2 t minced onion

Put ingredients in a bread machine or knead by hand and let it rise. Put in loaf pan. Bake at 350 for 30 minutes, or until loaf sounds hollow when tapped.

Dianne Wiebe

You could go a little heavier on the seasoning and onion, or add dried tomatoes, or a little parmesan cheese. My recipes are for the 1 ½ pound loaf, adjust quantities for larger loaves.

* * * * *

Laughter is brightest where food is best.
Irish Proverb

BANANA CHOCOLATE CHIP BREAD

¼ c margarine
1 ¼ c sugar
1 tsp vanilla
1 egg
1 ½ c mashed banana
½ c milk

2 c flour
1 tsp baking powder
½ tsp baking soda
½ c chopped nuts
½ pkg chocolate chips

Pre-heat oven to 350°. Cream margarine and sugar together. Add vanilla and egg. Mix well. Add banana and milk. Stir. Add remaining ingredients. Mix well. Bake in well greased loaf pan 30-40 minutes until knife inserted in center comes out clean. Let cool before removing from pan.

April Marl

BANANA-BRAN BREAD
(No Eggs)

¾ cup unsifted all purpose
  flour
¾ cup unsifted whole wheat
  flour
2 tsp baking powder
½ tsp baking soda
¼ tsp salt

¼ cup butter (½ stick)
¼ cup sugar
1 cup bran flakes (cereal)
1 ½ cups mashed ripe
  banana
2 Tbsp water
1 tsp vanilla

Mix all together. Pour into a greased loaf pan. Bake in a preheated 350°F oven for 55 minutes. Cool in pan on rack for 10 minutes. Remove from pan and cool.

Marie (Freddie) Peterson

BANANA NUT BREAD

2 cups flour
1 tsp baking soda
½ cup oleo or butter
¾ cup sugar
2 large eggs

1 cup nuts
1 ½ cup mashed bananas
  (about 3)
2 Tbsp hot water

Beat oleo and sugar until smooth and creamy, add eggs, stir in bananas and nuts. Add flour and baking soda (mixed) and stir well. Add hot water last and put in greased pan or 2 smaller ones. Bake in 350°F oven about 1 hour.

Chris Stedner

GALEN'S SURPRISE MUFFINS

(Our son, Galen came up with this variation on Blueberry Muffins when he was about 10.)

Dry:

2 cups Whole Wheat pastry flour (grain grown at Lightning Tree Farm Millbrook, NY and milled at Wild Hive Farm Bakery Clinton Corners, NY)

¾ cup unbleached white flour (or use all whole wheat pastry flour)
1 Tbsp baking powder
½ tsp salt

Wet:

2 eggs (from our chickens)
¼ cup butter, melted (or light oil)
½ cup honey (from No Hope Honey Funny Farm Newburgh, NY)

1 cup milk (from a local farm)
1 tsp vanilla

Berries:

¾ cup each blueberries and cranberries picked from the Shawangunk Ridge

(Blueberry season is July to August. Cranberries come just before the first hard frost. We freeze pickings to use all year round. If you use frozen berries, do not defrost- use straight from the freezer)

Grease muffin tins. Mix dry together. Mix wet together. If honey is hard, soften with butter/oil for 30 seconds in microwave or in a double boiler. Add wet to dry completely, but do not overmix. Stir in berries gently and evenly. Fill greased muffin tins. Bake 25-30 minutes or until a toothpick stuck in comes out clean.

Decadent Variation: instead of just berries, use ½ cup each: blueberries, cranberries and chocolate chips!

Liana Hoodes
Galen Church

REALLY GOOD PIE CRUST

1 ½ c flour   5-6 tbs ice water
10 ⅔ tbs. (⅔ cup) Butter
  (frozen)

    Add flour & cubed butter to Cuisinart, flash 6-8 times till beaded, add cold water while mixing into ball, then roll out and bake with or without filling depending on the pie you are making.

Don Schlesinger

* * * * *

How can you be expected to govern a country that has 246 kinds of cheese?

Charles de Gaulle

YOUR FAVORITE RECIPES

Recipe

BREADS & PASTRIES

DESSERTS

Purple Bearded Iris
Austa Densmore Sturdevant (1855-1936)

Recipe Favorites

Page No.

Recipe Title:_____

_____   _____
_____   _____
_____   _____
_____   _____
_____   _____
_____   _____
_____   _____
_____   _____
_____   _____
_____   _____

Family Favorites

Page No.

Recipe Title:_____

_____   _____
_____   _____
_____   _____
_____   _____
_____   _____

Notes:_____

_____
_____
_____

DESSERTS

CHOCOLATE ALMOND CRUNCH

Unsalted Saltines
2 sticks butter
1 cup brown sugar

12 oz. chocolate chips
½ cup chopped almonds

Line the bottom of a cookie sheet with sides with aluminum foil and grease it. Lay saltines evenly on sheet. In saucepan melt butter. Add brown sugar and boil 3 minutes. Pour mixture evenly over crackers; spread carefully. Bake 4 minutes at 400°F. Sprinkle chocolate chips over top. Shut oven off and return cookie sheet to oven for 3 minutes. Spread chips and sprinkle with chopped almonds. Wait until cool freeze for 1 hour. Break into pieces- Delicious!

Sally H. Matz

RUMBALLS

2 cups (1 pkg) Vanilla Wafers
(Keebler are best), ground
fine
1 cup walnuts or pecans,
ground fine

1 cup confectioners sugar
3 Tbsp dark cocoa
⅓ tsp salt
3 Tbsp corn syrup, light
¼- ⅓ cup rum or brandy

Mix ground vanilla wafers, nuts, confectioners sugar, cocoa and salt well. Add corn syrup and slowly add rum, mixing all the while. The mixture should be just moist enough to form small balls (small walnut size) but not soggy. Roll balls in granulated sugar and keep airtight container lined with wax paper- best are small round metal cookie bins. Enjoy!

Irene Seeland

* * * * *

The first zucchini I ever saw I killed it with a hoe.
John Gould

WHITE CHOCOLATE WHIPPED CREAM

2 oz. good quality white
chocolate, chopped
(Baker's or Lindt)

2 Tbsp ½ cup chilled
whipping cream

Combine Chopped white chocolate and 2 Tbsp whipping cream in small microwavable bowl. Microwave on high for 30 seconds. Stir until white chocolate melts and mixture is smooth. Cool white chocolate mixture 10 minutes. Beat remaining ½ cup chilled whipping cream in medium bowl until soft peaks form. Whisk in white chocolate mixture. (Can be prepared 1 day ahead.) Cover and refrigerate. Recipe can be doubled.

John Duncan

White chocolate adds depth to your usual whipped cream and will hold it's shape even when made in advance.

* * * * *

Custard: A detestable substance produced by a malevolent conspiracy of the hen, the cow, and the cook.
Ambrose Bierce, American Writer

PUMPKIN CHIFFON PIE

3 egg yolks, slightly beaten
½ c sugar (raw gives better
   flavor)
1 & ¼ c pumpkin
½ c milk
½ t salt
½ t ground ginger
½ t ground nutmeg

½ t ground cinnamon
1 envelope gelatin (or agar
   flakes if vegetarian)
3 egg whites or Just Whites,
   re-constituted to the
   equivalent
10" graham cracker crust,
   homemade or bought.

In a double boiler, heat the milk and sugar til hot, stirring frequently. Using a whisk, stirring constantly, drizzle in the beaten egg yolks. Add the pumpkin, salt and spices. Cook and stir frequently until the mixture is custard-like. In a small bowl, soften 1 envelope gelatin in ¼ cold water (if using agar, follow package directions). When pumpkin mixture is cooked, add gelatin (agar) and stir in til dissolved. Cool.

When the mixture is cool, but not set, beat the egg whites or the Just whites until stiff and dry. Slowly beat in ½ c (raw) sugar. Fold carefully into the thoroughly cooled pumpkin mixture. Scrape gently into the prepared graham cracker crust. Refrigerate. Best made the day before or early morning so that it has plenty of time to set before serving. Serve with lightly sweetened whipped cream.

Hattie Grifo
in memory of my mother, Harriet Woodruff

For a gluten-free alternative, just pour the mixture into an attractive serving dish and serve as a pudding, or make an alternative wheat/gluten-free crust with coconut or an alternative flour.

A Thanksgiving and Christmas favorite.

* * * * *

Love is a basket with five loaves and two fishes;
It's never enough until you start to give it away.

CRAZY ZZZZZZZZZ APPLE PIE

6-8 cups zucchini, peeled
   and sliced
1 cup sugar
¼ tsp nutmeg or allspice
½ tsp cinnamon
⅔ cup lemon juice

4 cups flour
1 ½ cup margarine
2 cups sugar
½ tsp salt
1 tsp cinnamon

Place zucchini, 1 cup sugar, lemon juice, ¼ tsp nutmeg or allspice and ½ tsp cinnamon in a large sauce pan and cook until tender, stirring occasionally to prevent sticking. Meanwhile mix flour, margarine, 2 cups sugar, salt and 1 tsp cinnamon. Mix together until the mixture resembles coarse crumbs. Reserve 1 cup for the topping and ½ cup to add to the zucchini mixture. Press the remaining crumbs into a 10x15 inch baking dish. Bake in a 375°F oven for 10 minutes. Mix the ½ cup crumbs with the zucchini mixture and spread this on the baked crust. Top with the remaining crumb mixture and bake for 30 minutes. Serves 12-16

Olga Weber

CHERRY TOP- CHEESE PIE

8 oz. cream cheese, softened
½ cup sugar
2 cups Cool Whip, thawed
1 can cherry pie filling

1 tsp almond flavoring
1 9 inch graham cracker
   crust

Blend sugar into softened cream cheese. Add almond flavoring. Blend in Cool Whip. Pour into graham cracker crust. Top with 1 cup cherry pie filling. Chill at least 3 hours before serving.

Audrey Keir

* * * * *

Without my morning coffee I'm just like a dried up piece of roast goat.

Johann Sebastian Bach

LAND'S END BLUEBERRY PIE

1 pt. blueberries
1 cup sugar
1 Tbsp flour
1 Tbsp tapioca

½ Tbsp lemon juice
prepared, or frozen, baked
  pie shell

Mix sugar, flour, tapioca, berries and lemon juice. Cook slowly over low heat until quite thick. Cool to lukewarm. Pour into baked pie shell. Add 1 pt blueberries on top. Press lightly into cooked mixture. Garnish with whipped cream.

Lois Colucci

* * * * *

If this is coffee, please bring me some tea; if this is tea, please bring me some coffee.

Abraham Lincoln

RHUBARB PIE

double pie crust (Everyone has his or her own pie crust- please use your own. Sometimes I like to use a pate sucre to add a little sweetness.)

3 cups rhubarb, diced uniformly (only the red stalks)

1 cup sugar

3 Tbsp Minute Tapioca (do not substitute any other kind of tapioca)

2 Tbsp butter, diced

milk and sugar

Preheat oven to 400°F. Place rack in the center of the oven. In a bowl mix together the diced rhubarb, 1 cup of sugar and the 3 Tbsp of Minute Tapioca. Set aside. Place 1 pie crust in a 9 inch pie pan, gently pressing into the pie pan. Add rhubarb mixture with the 2 Tbsp of diced butter. Lay the other pie crust gently on top and press edges together. Next, lightly brush some milk all over the pie crust, and then sprinkle it with sugar. This gives it a beautiful color and adds a little sweetness. Score the pie crust with a knife, making at least 5 small slits (make a fun design if you wish) so that a little steam can escape. Bake for 40-50 minutes, until golden brown on the top and bottom. Cool on a rack. I like to eat it slightly warm, with a little vanilla ice cream or whipped cream!

Katie McDevitt

This recipe came from a Betty Crocker cookbook my Grandma Bertsch received as a shower gift in 1959. It is my Grandpa's favorite. My mom likes to add 1 tbsp of Grand Marnier and 1 tsp of orange zest for a little kick!

* * * * *

Anybody can make you enjoy the first bite of a dish, but only a real chef can make you enjoy the last.

Francois Minot

KEY LIME PIE

1 box (0.3 oz) Sugar-Free
   Lime flavor gelatin
¼ cup boiling water
2 containers (8 oz.) each Key
   Lime Pie flavor light
   yogurt

1 container (8 oz.) frozen
   fat-free whipped topping,
   thawed
1 prepared 9 in. reduced-fat
   graham cracker pie crust

In a large bowl dissolve gelatin in boiling water. Stir in yogurt with a wire whisk. Fold in topping with wooden spoon. Put mixture in graham cracker crust; refrigerate overnight or 2 hours. Serves 8.

Joyce Stedner

* * * * *

What you see before you, my friend, is the result of a lifetime of chocolate...

Katherine Hepburn

BLUEBERRY BUTTERMILK TART

Pie Shell:

1 ⅓ C flour
¼ C sugar
¼ t salt
1 stick (½ C) cold unsalted
   butter, cut into bits

1 large egg yolk beaten with
   2 T ice water
raw rice for weighting the
   shell

Filling:

1 C buttermilk
3 large egg yolks
½ C granulated sugar
1 T freshly grated lemon zest
1 T fresh lemon juice
½ stick (¼ C) unsalted
   butter, melted and cooled

1 t vanilla
½ t salt
2 T all purpose flour
2 C picked-over blueberries
confectioners' sugar for
   sprinkling the tart

Pie Shell: In a bowl, stir together flour, sugar and salt; add butter and blend the mixture until it resembles coarse meal. Add the yolk mixture and toss the mixture until the liquid is incorporated, and form the dough into a ball. Dust the dough with flour and chill it, wrapped in plastic wrap, for 1 hour. Roll out dough ⅛ inch thick on a floured surface, fit it into a 10 inch tart pan with a removable fluted rim, and chill the shell for at least 30 minutes, or covered overnight. Line the shell with foil, fill the foil with rice, and bake the shell in the middle of a preheated 350 oven for 25 minutes. Remove the foil and rice carefully, bake the shell for 5 to 10 minutes more, or until it is pale golden, and let it cool in the pan on a rack.

Filling: Preheat oven to 350. In blender or food processor, blend together buttermilk, yolks, granulated sugar, zest, lemon juice, butter, vanilla, salt and flour until the mixture is smooth; spread blueberries evenly over the bottom of the shell, and pour the buttermilk mixture over them. Bake the tart in the middle of the oven on a baking sheet lined with foil (in case of run-over) for 30 to 35 minutes, or until the filling is just set.

Let the tart cool completely in pan on the rack; sprinkle it with confectioners' sugar, sifted, and serve at room temperature or chilled, with blueberry ice cream (see following recipe).

John Duncan

COUSIN TERRY JOHNSON'S GREEK PUDDING

1¼ c. rice
1 gal. whole milk
5 eggs

2½ c. sugar
1 Tbsp. vanilla (or more)
ground cinnamon

1. Bring milk to a boil in a very large pot, stirring often. Be careful that it doesn't boil over.
2. Add rice and 1 ¼ c. sugar. Continue stirring until mixture comes to a boil again; then turn down heat and simmer until rice is soft, about 1 hour, stirring occasionally so mixture doesn't scorch.
3. In meantime thoroughly combine eggs and remaining sugar.
4. When rice is soft, add egg mixture and cook 5 or 10 minutes, until thickened. Cool slightly and add vanilla.
5. Pour into large pan and cover with lots of ground cinnamon. Cover with plastic wrap and let set overnight.

David McAlpin

This was a specialty of the Johnson's restaurant in Bourbonnais, IL. The restaurant closed years ago, but the pudding remains a winner.

DOROTHY OAKES' RICE PUDDING

1 qt milk
¼ c raw rice
½ c sugar
½ t salt

½ c raisins (optional)
1 t vanilla
¼ t nutmeg

Preheat oven to 300°.

Mix milk, rice, sugar and salt in buttered casserole dish. Bake uncovered 2 hours, stirring every ½ hour. Add (raisins), vanilla and nutmeg, and bake ½ hour longer, without stirring, or until rice is tender.

**Hattie Grifo, Director, in memory
of Dorothy Oakes, previous Director**

BERRY RICE PUDDING

(Used by permission from "Sara's Secrets for Weeknight Meals", Broadway Books, 2005.)

I love rice pudding, as does the husband, but I am certainly not going to make it from scratch on a week night. However, there is a good chance you have leftover rice every so often from a take-out meal, and this would be a very tasty way to recycle it.

1 ½ cups cooked leftover
   long-grain white rice
½ cup ginger marmalade
½ cup heavy cream
2 teaspoons vanilla extract

1 pint blueberries, rinsed
   and dried
1 pint raspberries, rinsed
   and dried

Combine the rice, marmalade, 2 tablespoons of the cream, and the vanilla in a large bowl. Beat the remaining cream in a small bowl with an electric beater until soft peaks form. Stir the whipped cream into the rice mixture.

Reserve 8 large blueberries and 8 large raspberries. Gently stir the remaining berries into the rice mixture and transfer to a serving bowl. Garnish with the reserved berries and serve or cover and refrigerate until ready to serve.

Makes about 6 servings.

Hands-on time: 10 minutes.

Total preparation time: 10 minutes.

Sara Moulton

Sara Moulton is host of the PBS show, "Sara's Weeknight Meals", executive chef Gourmet Magazine and food editor, Good Morning America.

* * * * *

Research tells us fourteen out of any ten individuals like chocolate.

Sandra Boynton

BLUEBERRY BUCKLE

¾ cup sugar
¼ cup butter or margarine
1 egg
½ cup milk

2 cups flour
2 tsp baking powder
½ tsp salt
2 cups blueberries

Topping:

½ cup sugar
⅓ cup flour

½ tsp cinnamon
¼ cup soft butter

Mix ingredients for topping together and set aside. Mix thoroughly: ¾ cup sugar, ¼ cup margarine and egg. Stir in milk. Sift together flour, baking powder and salt. Add to the creamed mixture. Carefully fold in 2 cups well-drained blueberries. Spread into a greased 9x13 inch pan. Sprinkle with topping. Bake in a 350°F oven for 30-40 minutes or until a toothpick inserted in center comes out clean.

Audrey Keir

PEACH & BERRY KUCHEN

(with gluten-free adaptation)

½ c butter
2 c flour (or 2 & ¾ c. rice
   flour + ¼ c tapioca flour)
¼ t baking powder
½ t salt
1 c heavy cream
1 c raw or brown sugar

12 peach halves or 2
   packages frozen slices
1 c each raspberries and
   blueberries (or more)
2 egg yolks, or 2 whole eggs,
   beaten
1 t cinnamon

Cut butter into flour, baking powder, salt, and 2 T sugar with pastry cutter or in a food processor until it looks like coarse meal. Press firmly, but not too firmly, into buttered 8 x 8 inch baking dish. Arrange peaches on the surface to cover, then sprinkle the berries in the crevices in between the peaches. Sprinkle fruit with mixture of cinnamon and remaining sugar. Bake 15 minutes at 400°. Beat egg yolks/eggs into the cream and pour over the top, and bake 40 minutes longer at 375°.

Hattie & Jack Grifo

You may use other fruits. Sour cream may be substituted for heavy cream.

APPLE PIE/COFFEE CAKE

1 pkg yellow cake mix
1 can apple pie filling
3 eggs
¾ cup sour cream
¼ cup water

2 Tbsp canola oil
1 tsp almond extract
2 Tbsp brown sugar
1 ½ tsp cinnamon

Mix topping using brown sugar, cinnamon and 1 ½ Tbsp of the yellow cake mix. Set aside. Combine eggs, sour cream, water, oil, almond extract and rest of cake mix. Mix at medium speed for 2 minutes. Add ½ can apple pie filling.

Spread ½ batter in greased 9x13 inch pan or 10 inch tube pan. Add remaining batter, rest of pie filling and then the topping mixture. Bake in the oven at 350°F for 30-45 minutes. Test with toothpick in center. It's done when the toothpick comes out clean. Dust with powdered sugar when cool or grizzle with a glaze.

Audrey Keir

APPLE SPOON DESSERT

4 cups (4 medium) apples,
  peeled and sliced
½ cup sugar
1 Tbsp flour

½ tsp cinnamon
¼ tsp nutmeg
2 Tbsp lemon juice

Topping:

¾ cup flour
½ cup sugar
¼ tsp baking soda
¼ tsp salt

¼ cup margarine
¼ cup milk
1 egg

Combine apples, sugar, flour, cinnamon, nutmeg and lemon juice. Place in 9 inch pan. In large mixing bowl, combine all topping ingredients at lowest speed until dry ingredients are moistened. Beat at high speed 2 minutes. Drop topping by spoonfuls over apple mixture- spread carefully. Bake at 350°F for 35-40 minutes until golden brown.

Lois Colucci

TOP OF THE STOVE APPLE BETTY

½ cup brown sugar
3 slices bread, diced
¼ cup butter

1 tsp cinnamon
1 cup applesauce
whipped cream or Cool Whip

In a sauce pan melt butter, add cinnamon, applesauce and brown sugar. Stir until all blended, then add cubed bread. Serve with whipped cream or Cool Whip. Quick and easy dessert.

Marie Stanger

MIMSIE'S APPLE CAKE

1 & ¼ cups cooking oil
  (canola, safflower)
3 eggs
2 c sugar
2 t vanilla
3 cups flour

1 t baking soda
2 t cinnamon
½ t salt
3 to 4 c chunked, fresh
  apples

Preheat oven to 325°.

Mix together dry ingredients. Beat together oil, eggs, and vanilla. Mix all ingredients together. Add the fresh apple chunks.

Turn mixture into an ungreased 9 or 10" tube pan. Bake for 1 & ½ hours or until done. Cool a few minutes in pan, then turn out onto a cooling rack, right side up.

Hattie Grifo in honor of Mims Grifo who used to live in Cragsmoor.

Apple chunks can be about ½ to 1" in size.

* * * * *

Eat breakfast like a king, lunch like a prince, and dinner like a pauper

Adelle Davis

AUNT MABEL'S CRANBERRY PIE CAKE

1 cup uncooked cranberries   ¾ cup chopped walnuts
¼ cup sugar

Batter:

1 egg   2 Tbsp vegetable oil
¾ cup sugar   ½ cup flour
¼ cup melted butter

Spread cranberries in a greased pie tin. Sprinkle with walnuts and sugar. In a bowl beat the egg, add sugar. Gradually add melted butter and oil. Mix well. Add flour. Mix well again. Pour batter over cranberries. Bake at 325°F for 40 minutes. Serve warm or cold with whipped cream or ice cream.

JoAnne Lindsley

BLUEBERRY CAKE

Cake:

2 cups sifted flour   ¼ cup butter
2 tsp baking powder   1 egg
½ tsp salt   ½ cup milk
1 cup sugar   2 ½ cups blueberries

Topping:

¼ cup butter   ¼ cup flour
½ cup brown sugar   ½ tsp cinnamon

For Cake: In a large bowl cream butter, add sugar, beat in egg and mix milk in. In a separate bowl sift flour, add salt and baking powder. Add to liquid. Beat until smooth. Fold in blueberries. Pour into greased, floured 9x9 inch pan.

For Topping: Cream butter, add sugar, add flour and cinnamon. Sprinkle over batter. Bake at 375°F. Check at 30 minutes. Should be golden on top.

Elfi Roze-Avinger

STRAWBERRY SHORTCAKE, KEELIN STYLE

1 recipe pie pastry, your
  favorite recipe
1 qt. fresh strawberries

sugar to taste
½ pt. heavy cream (optional)
1 tsp. vanilla extract

1. Roll out pie dough, cut into approximately 3" squares. place on cookie sheet and bake at 425 until lightly browned and crisp. Remove carefully to rack and let cool.
2. Clean strawberries and place in mixing bowl. With potato masher or similar tool, smush the berries. Add sugar to taste.
3. Whip cream, sweeten lightly to taste and add vanilla. Put in serving bowl.
4. At serving time, layer pie crust squares and smashed berries in individual bowls. Serve with whipped cream to accompany.

David McAlpin

David's mother's family recipe, from southern Illinois. The berries are enhanced by the pie crust, which isn't as doughy as the more usual biscuit.

* * * * *

Red meat is not bad for you. Now blue-green meat, that's bad for you!

Tommy Smothers

PINEAPPE SOUR CREAM CAKE

1 20 oz can crushed pineapple in syrup (it is sometimes hard to find these days, you can use the pineapple packed in juice)
3 cups flour
2 cups sugar
1 tsp baking soda
3 eggs lightly beaten

1 cup sour cream or plain yogurt
¾ cup vegetable oil
1 Tbsp vanilla (tablespoon is correct)
1 Tbsp grated fresh lemon peel (orange peel is good too)

Drain syrup or juice from pineapple. Set aside. In large mixing bowl, stir flour, sugar and soda to blend. Make a well in center of dry ingredients. In another bowl, combine eggs, sour cream, pineapple, oil, vanilla and lemon/orange peel. Add all at once to dry ingredients. Stir until just moist. Pour into greased and floured 10 inch tube pan or Bundt pan. Bake 65-70 minutes at 350°F. Cool in pan 20 minutes. Gently loosen with spatula. Place a plate upside down on top of the baking pan and turn both upside down so the cake falls gently onto plate. Cool

Note: This cake is fine by itself, but a quick glaze can be made by mixing together some powdered sugar and left over pineapple juice and maybe a dash of lemon juice into a runny consistency and drizzling over the cake with a spoon. Alternately, the left over juice can be put in a small saucepan with some sugar and heated until the sugar melts. Punch holes in the cake with a toothpick and pour it over the cake for a more dense and moist cake. Or both!

Anonymous

* * * * *

My mother's menu consisted of two choices: Take it or leave it.

Buddy Hackett

SPICED NECTARINE CAKE

1 stick butter (½ cup)
¾ cup plus 1 Tbsp sugar
2 large eggs
1 Tbsp lemon juice
1 ½ tsp lemon peel (orange or tangerine is great too!)
1 ¼ cup SELF RISING FLOUR (not regular flour)
5 medium nectarines (1 ¾ lb) sliced (or a little less and throw in some blueberries)
¾ tsp cinnamon

Butter 9 inch spring-form pan. Beat butter in large bowl until fluffy. Add ¾ cup sugar; beat until blended. Beat in one egg at a time, then lemon juice and peel. Beat in flour until smooth. Spread batter in pan. Arrange nectarines to cover completely; press in lightly to adhere. Mix 3 Tbsp sugar and ¾ tsp cinnamon and sprinkle over cake. Bake in 350°F until cake is golden and toothpick comes out clean. About one hour. Cut around cake to loosen. Remove pan. Serve warm or at room temperature. Great warm with whipped cream or vanilla ice cream topping it all off!

Anonymous

Worth buying a spring form pan for this yummy recipe that gets a work out in the summer!

ECLAIR CAKE

1 stick butter
1 cup water
1 cup all purpose flour
4 large eggs
1 8 oz. pkg cream cheese, softened
2 boxes (3.4 oz.) instant pudding mix
1 8 oz. container frozen whipped topping, thawed
4 cups milk (your choice)
Chocolate syrup

Heat oven to 425°F. Coat 13x9x2 in. baking dish with nonstick cooking spray. In a medium saucepan, melt butter, add water and flour. Cook until dough forms a ball. Remove from heat. Add eggs, one at a time. Spread into prepared baking dish. Bake for 20 minutes. Remove from oven and press down center. Make pudding as directed on package, adding the softened cream cheese. Spread pudding mixture on crust. Top with whipped topping. Drizzle with chocolate syrup. Serve cold.

Judy Rode

CHUMBOLONE

(Italian Pound Cake)

5 cups flour
5 tea spoon baking powder
1 c sugar
1 c milk

2 sticks butter
5 eggs
2 tsp Anisette

Mix eggs & sugar. Add milk. Alternate flour & baking powder. Mix well. Add flavoring & melted butter. Bake in well greased tube pan @ 350° 1 hr.

Angelina Capobianco
Grandmother of Mary Ann Maurer

Great toasted.

MADLYN'S POUND CAKE

2 sticks sweet butter
¼ c. vegetable shortening
  (yes)
2½ c. sugar
5 eggs

1 Tbsp. vanilla extract
1 tsp. lemon extract
1 c. milk
3 c. flour

1. Have eggs and shortening at room temperature.
2. Oven at 350. Grease and flour 10" tube pan.
3. Cream butter, shortening and sugar until very pale colored and fluffy.
4. Add extracts and beat well.
5. Beat in eggs, one by one.
6. Alternately add flour and milk till well blended.
7. Pour into pan, bake 1¼ to 1½ hours till cake tests done. Immediately remove from pan and let cool on rack.

Mary Kroul McAlpin

The best pound cake ever.

* * * * *

Only two things in this world are too serious to be jested on, potatoes and matrimony.

Irish Saying

CHOCOLATE CAKE
(No Eggs)

2 cups sugar
3 cups all purpose flour
2 tsp baking soda
1 tsp salt
½ cup cocoa

¾ cup oil
2 Tbsp vinegar
2 cups cold water
1 tsp vanilla

Mix together all dry ingredients. Mix in wet ingredients. Bake in a greased 9x13x2 inch pan in a 350°F oven for 25-30 minutes.

Marie (Freddie) Peterson

This recipe was made for 2, 000 students at the University of Puget Sound College where I worked. I cut it down to family cake.

GINGERBREAD CAKE

2 ½ cups flour
½ cup sugar
1 ½ tsp baking soda
¾ tsp salt (omit if using
    salted butter)
1 tsp cinnamon

1 tsp ginger
½ tsp cloves
½ cup butter
1 cup water
1 cup molasses
1 egg

In one bowl soften butter and blend all other ingredients together. Pour into a greased loaf or Bundt cake pan (the cake pan works very well with this recipe). Bake at 350°F for about 40 minutes.

Food tip: Ginger and chocolate are complimentary.... so.... chocolate frosting is STRONGLY recommended!

Frosting Recipe: Melt 2 squares unsweetened chocolate on low heat. Measure 2 ½ cups confectioners sugar into a bowl. Stir in melted chocolate. Add in milk 1 Tbsp at a time mixing it in until frosting is of desired thickness.

**Elizabeth Santoli
Irene Dunn**

PUMPKIN PATCH CAKE ROLL

Cake:

3 eggs, separated
¾ cup brown sugar
½ cup pumpkin
¾ cup flour
½ tsp. baking powder

½ tsp. baking soda
½ tsp. ground cinnamon
¼ tsp. salt
¼ tsp. ground cloves

Preheat oven to 350°F. In a small mixing bowl, beat egg yolks with mixer or whisk until thick (about 5 minutes). Gradually add sugar, beating well. Stir in pumpkin. Sift together dry ingredients; fold into egg mixture. Beat egg whites until stiff peaks form. Fold in to batter.

Spread batter evenly onto greased and floured cookie sheet lined with wax paper. (Use a cookie sheet approx. 15 ½ x 10 x 1.) Bake 14-18 minutes on middle rack. Immediately loosen sides of cake. Invert onto clean dish towel lightly dusted with powdered sugar. Remove wax paper and starting from the narrow end, roll cake in towel. Cool on wire rack, unroll cake and spread with cream cheese filling.

Filling:

1 8 oz. package cream
  cheese, softened
8 tbls. butter, softened

1 cup sifted powdered sugar
1 tsp. vanilla extract

Combine cream cheese and butter. Cream until fluffy. Gradually add powdered sugar and butter; beat until well blended. Spread over cooled, unrolled cake. Re-roll, slice and serve.

OPTIONAL: Make extra filling and use it to ice the cake or frost with chocolate frosting.

Lori Stehlin

* * * * *

A world without tomatoes is like a string quartet without violins.

Laurie Colwin, Home Cooking

ENHANCED ANGEL FOOD CAKE

To 1 store bought Angle food cake mix add:

1 tsp cinnamon
¼ tsp nutmeg

¼ tsp clove

Mix according to box instructions and cook.

Glaze:

1 c confectioners sugar
2 tbs OJ

1 tbs grated OJ peel

Mix the three ingredients together. When the cake is out of the pan and cool. Spread the glaze over the top of the cake and let it run down the sides.

Don Schlesinger

NEW ENGLAND SPIDER CAKE

2 cups milk
4 tsp vinegar
¾ cup corn meal
1 cup all purpose flour (or ½ cup whole wheat and ½ cup all purpose for more fiber)
¾ cup sugar (use less for less sweetness)

½ tsp baking soda
½ tsp salt
2 eggs
1 cup heavy cream (use evaporated milk to cut fat)
2 tbls butter (or non-stick spray to cut fat)

Preheat oven 350°F.

Combine milk and vinegar. Set aside to sour in a large bowl. Combine dry ingredients in a bowl. Whisk eggs into sour milk and add dry ingredients.

Melt butter in a 12 inch cast-iron skillet (or round frying pan). Pour in batter, then pour cream into the center and slide skillet in the oven. Bake until golden brown on top; about 45 minutes. Cut into wedges while warm and serve with fruit or jam. This is also good reheated.

Mary Davidson

MILKY WAY CAKE AND FROSTING

Cake:

13 small Milky Way bars (fun size)	1 ½ cups flour
2 sticks butter	½ tsp baking soda
2 cups sugar	1 ¼ buttermilk
4 eggs	1 tsp vanilla
	1 cup nuts

Preheat oven to 350°F. Melt butter and Milky Way bars together over low heat, stirring constantly. Add sugar and beat well with electric mixer. Beat in eggs, flour, soda, buttermilk, and vanilla. Stir in nuts. Pour into greased/floured Bundt pan. Bake at 350°F for 1 hour and 20 minutes. Cool and frost.

Frosting:

6 small Milky Way bars (fun size)	2 Tbsp milk
1 stick butter	1 tsp vanilla
	1 cup powdered sugar

Melt butter and Milky Way bars together on low heat, stirring constantly. Add milk, vanilla and sifted powdered sugar.

Note: Use a sifter or strainer to add some of the powdered sugar when melting the bars/butter because if it is all added together at the end, there is a tendency for it to get lumpy, but sifting the sugar helps as does strong stirring!

Anonymous

This Frosted cake is even better the next day!

* * * * *

It's difficult to think anything but pleasant thoughts while eating a homegrown tomato.

Lewis Grizzard

AUNT MARTHA'S RED VELVET CAKE

1 ½ oz red food coloring (2
 small bottles)
2 tbs cocoa
1 ½ c sugar
1 c butter
2 eggs

2 ½ c sifted baking flour
½ tsp salt
1 ½ tsp baking soda
1 c buttermilk
1 tsp vanilla
1 tbs vinegar

Preheat oven to 350°.

Mix cocoa and coloring and let it stand. Cream butter & sugar, then add eggs and mix. Sift all dry ingredients together. Alternately add to dry ingredients the buttermilk and cocoa mixture.

Beat together (use electric mixer or 200 strokes by hand. Then stir in vanilla and vinegar. Grease and flour 8 or 9 inch cake pans. Bake @ 350° for 35 minutes.

Martha Capobianco

JOANNE'S BANANA BIRTHDAY CAKE

2 ¼ cups flour
½ tsp baking powder
¾ tsp baking soda
½ tsp salt
½ cup butter
1 ½ cups sugar

2 eggs
1 ¼ cups banana, mashed
2 tsp vanilla
¼ cup yogurt
1 ¼ cups walnuts, finely
 chopped

Sift together dry ingredients. Cream butter, eggs and sugar. Combine separately bananas, yogurt and vanilla. Take all three mixtures and combine them together, a little at a time, until smooth. Fold in walnuts. Bake in two 9 inch pans at 350°F for 30 minutes. Make a buttercream frosting by whipping together ½ cups butter and 8 oz. of cream cheese. Add in 3 cups powdered sugar, 2 tsp vanilla, and 2 Tbsp maple syrup. Make icing the cake, put a layer of sliced bananas sprinkled with lemon juice in the center and decorate with mint leaves, which add a unique flavor. This recipe also works well for cupcakes. Reduce the baking time to about 20 minutes and cut the frosting recipe in half

Bethany Lindsley

BELOVED BIRTHDAY CAKE

Cake:

4 oz baking chocolate
4 Tbsp unsalted butter
2 eggs
2 cups sugar
2 tsp vanilla

2 cups cold water
2 ½ cups flour
2 tsp baking soda
½ tsp salt

Melt chocolate in a double boiler. In a large bowl beat eggs. Slowly add sugar. Add melted chocolate. Add vanilla. Add cold water. Beat until smooth. Sift together flour, baking soda and salt. Add all at once to chocolate mixture. Beat with an eggbeater until smooth. Bake in 2 grease 9 inch cake pans for 40 minutes at 350°F. When cake had cooled, cover with icing.

Icing:

2 sticks room temperature
  butter
3 egg yolks

3 cups confectioners sugar
1 tsp vanilla

Mash butter and egg yolks together. Mix well. Add sugar gradually. Mix until smooth. Add vanilla. Finish mixing and frost cake.

Laura Hughes

* * * * *

I refuse to believe that trading recipes is silly. Tunafish casserole is at least as real as corporate stock.
Barbara Grizzuti Harrison

BLACK BOTTOM CUPCAKES

Cake Mixture:

1 ½ cups flour	⅓ cup cooking oil
1 cup sugar	1 tsp vinegar
½ cup cocoa	1 tsp vanilla
1 tsp baking soda	1 cup boiling water
½ tsp salt	

Cream Cheese Filling:

1 8 oz. cream cheese	½ cup sugar
1 3 oz. cream cheese	1 ½ cups chocolate chips
1 egg	

Put flour, 1 cup sugar, cocoa, baking soda and salt in a mixing bowl. Add boiling water and mix. Then add oil, vinegar and vanilla. In separate bowl mix all of the cream cheese, egg and ½ cup sugar. Blend well and add chocolate chips. Put 1 tsp of cake mixture, in liners, in midget size muffin pan. Top with 1 tsp cream cheese filling. Bake at 350°F for 12-15 minutes.

Fay Horn

* * * * *

Health food may be good for the conscience but Oreos taste a heck of a lot better.

Robert Redford

DUNCAN'S GROWN-UP BROWNIE'S

8 oz. unsweetened chocolate
8 oz. (2 sticks) unsalted
   butter
5 eggs
1 Tbsp vanilla extract
1 tsp almond extract
¼ tsp salt

2 ½ Tbsp dry instant
   espresso powder
½ tsp ground cinnamon
3 ¾ cup sugar
1-⅔ cup sifted all purpose
   flour
8 oz. (2 generous cups)
   walnut or pecan pieces

Preheat oven to 425°F. Place rack ⅓ up from bottom of oven. Line 9x13x2 inch baking pan with aluminum foil. Brush with melted butter. Melt and blend chocolate and butter in a microwave (covered) or on low heat in a heavy saucepan. Do not overheat.

In a large bowl, use an electric mixer to beat the eggs with vanilla, almond, salt, espresso powder, cinnamon, and sugar at high speed for 10 minutes. At low speed, add chocolate mixture and flour only until it is mixed. Stir in nuts.

Bake for 35 minutes. It will have a thick crusty top, but will be moist in the center. Not to worry- it is done. Cool brownies on a rack at room temperature. Invert onto rack and remove foil. Invert back to "top side up". Brownies should rest 6-8 hours before cutting into squares. Use a wet serrated knife. Makes 24 generous servings.

John Duncan

A very rich and often requested brownie recipe in Cragsmoor. Best made the day before serving.

* * * * *

You don't have to cook fancy or complicated masterpieces just good food from fresh ingredients.
Julia Child

SURPRISE BROWNIES

1 pkg German chocolate
   cake mix (do not add
   ingredients on the box)
⅓ cup evaporated milk

¾ cup butter or margarine
   (melted)
¾ cup pecans
14 oz. pkg Kraft caramels
6 oz. chocolate chips

Mix first 3 ingredients. Spread ½ mixture in 9x12 inch pan. Bake at 350°F for 15 minutes. Sprinkle in baked half, chocolate chips and cut-up pecans. Melt caramels with evaporated milk in a double-boiler. Pour over chips and nuts. Crumble other half of cake mixture over everything. Bake at 350°F for 15 minutes.

Fay Horn

CHOCOLATE TIRAMISU

10 EGG YOLKS
½ CUP SUGAR
1 lb SEMI-SWEET
   CHOCOLATE, MELTED
1 tbsp. VANILLA EXTRACT
¼ CUP MARSALA WINE
1 lb MASCARPONE CHEESE

¾ QUART HEAVY CREAM,
   BEATEN STIFF PEAKS
24 LADY FINGER COOKIES
3 CUPS WARM ESPRESSO
   COFFEE
½ CUP SIMPLE SYRUP
COCOA POWDER FOR
   DUSTING

PLACE YOLKS, SUGAR, VANILLA AND WINE IN AN ELECTRIC MIXING BOWL WITH THE WHIP. BEAT ON MEDIUM HIGH SPEED UNTIL CREAMY. ADD CHOCOLATE AND MIX. ADD MASCARPONE CHEESE AND MIX ONLY UNTIL INCORPORATED. DO NOT OVER MIX! SCRAP BOWL AND PUT ASIDE BEAT CREAM UNTIL STIFF PEAKS FOLD IN WHIPPED CREAM INTO MASCARPONE CREAM VERY GENTLY LINE GLASS BOWL WITH ½ OF THE CREAM SOAK LADY FINGERS IN THE COFFEE SYRUP AND LAY ABOVE THE FIRST LAYER OF CREAM, SPREAD THE REMAINING CREAM ON TOP OF THE COOKIES, SMOOTHING COMPLETELY FINISH WITH SIFTED COCOA POWDER.

Sandy Ingber

Sandy Ingber is Chef of the Oyster Bar in Grand Central Station NYC

SIMPLE TRIFLE

2 pkg vanilla pudding (not
   instant)
4 cups milk
1 pt heavy cream

½ cup sugar
1 16 oz. can fruit cocktail
1 pkg Lady Fingers or
   sponge cake

Make pudding according to directions and let cool. Whip cream, beat in ½ cup sugar to 1 ½ cups cream and chill. Drain fruit cocktail. Combine pudding, fruit and ½ whipped cream. Mix well. Layer ½ pudding mixture, a layer of cake, and then the rest of the pudding. Top with the reserved whipped cream and chill.

Nancy Krom

QUICK TRIFLE

2 small pound cakes
1 large package pudding mix
1 large cool whip
3 c milk

1 ½ jars jam (raspberry or
   orange marmalade or use
   pie filling)
1 bag sliced almonds, toasted
¼ to ½ bottle sherry

Slice the pound cake. Make the pudding using the milk. Layer all ingredients in glass bowl, sprinkle the layers with sherry. Refrigerate for several hours before serving. Makes one large & one small trifle.

Dianne Wiebe

AUNT STELLA'S ANISE COOKIES

4 eggs
1 c sugar
½ c vegetable oil

2 ½ c flour
1 tbs baking powder
1 tsp anise flavor

Sift dry ingredients together. Mix in other ingredients one at a time until blended. Drop cookies by the spoonful on a baking sheet and bake at 350 for 25 minutes.

Stella Capobianco Jones

CHOCOLATE CHIP COOKIES

4 ½ cups flour
2 tsp baking soda
1 tsp salt
1 cup softened butter/soy
  margarine (do not melt)
1 cup shortening

1 cup firmly packed brown
  sugar
1 cup sugar
4 eggs
2 tsp vanilla extract
chocolate chips (12 oz or
  more)

Preheat oven to 350°F. Cream sugars with butter and shortening. Beat eggs and vanilla together and add to creamed mixture. Mix until smoothed. Mix dry ingredients together separately and add to other mixture. If too moist, add more flour 1 tbls at a time to firm up. Add chocolate chips mixing by hand. Bake approximately 11 minutes.

Lori Stehlin

WALNUT BALL COOKIES

1 lb butter
8 tbs sugar
4 tsp of vanilla

4 cups of flour
2 - 3 c coarsely chopped
  walnuts

Mix all ingredients together by hand until the mixture is crumbly. Roll into small balls. Place on cookie sheets and bake in 375 oven until just slightly brown. Cool. Put some powdered sugar in a bag and shake 5 - 6 cookies in the sugar until coated. Repeat until all are coated. Makes 70 -75 cookies

Jeane Noud

* * * * *

An onion can make people cry, but there has never been a vegetable invented to make them laugh.

Will Rogers

BLUEBERRY ICE CREAM

2 C picked-over blueberries   1 C milk
¾ C sugar   1 ½ C heavy cream
⅛ t salt

In saucepan, bring blueberries, sugar and salt to a boil over moderate heat, mashing berries and stirring with a fork. Simmer mixture, stirring frequently, 5 minutes and cool slightly. In blender, puree mixture with milk just until smooth and stir in cream. Pour puree through a sieve into a bowl, pressing on solids with back of a spoon. Chill mixture, covered, at least 2 hours, or until cold, and up to 1 day.

Freeze mixture in an ice-cream maker. Transfer ice cream to an airtight container and put in freezer to harden. Ice cream may be made 1 week ahead.

John Duncan

* * * * *

I will not eat oysters. I want my food dead. Not sick, not wounded, dead.

Woody Allen

Rose bouquet
Austa Densmore Sturdevant (1855-1936)

Recipe Favorites

Page No.

Recipe Title:_____ _____

_____ _____

_____ _____

_____ _____

_____ _____

_____ _____

_____ _____

_____ _____

_____ _____

_____ _____

Family Favorites

Page No.

Recipe Title:_____ _____

_____ _____

_____ _____

_____ _____

_____ _____

_____ _____

Notes:_____

_____

_____

702-08

MISCELLANEOUS

GINNY'S ICED TEA

The way this has evolved in our family, where it's a staple, is:

⅓ c. loose tea (I use Brooke Bond Red Label, a good Darjeeling available at Indian groceries)

1 qt. (approximately) water
1 can frozen lemonade, thawed

Bring water just to a boil and brew tea. Allow tea to cool. Pour off tea and discard leaves. (Original recipe used 6 to 8 tea bags.) Pour tea into ½ gal. pitcher, add thawed lemonade, mix. Divide mixture between 2, ½ gal. pitchers, fill each with water and mix again. Refrigerate.

Mary Kroul McAlpin

This is a fascinating case of the wonderful continuity of little things.

My mother, Leni Kroul, got the original recipe sometime in the late 1950s from her friend, Virginia (Ginny) Abrahamsen, who lived half a mile from where we then summered, between Wallkill and Gardiner. The Abrahamsens had a dairy farm and six kids (and the hired man had five more), so it was a fascinating place for an only child from New York City, and one of the girls was my "summer best friend." Rebekah Leonard just happens to be Ginny's granddaughter.

In that place and that time, the standard summer drink for kids was Kool-Aid, which sold 5 for 10 cents; A&P's Cheeri-Aid was 6 for a dime, if one needed to economize. We kids claimed to be able to detect the "real thing". Grape, cherry, even fruit punch (anything red) were pretty good; root beer, lime and lemon or lemonade flavors were yucky.

This ice tea blew all other warm weather drinks out of the water, including ice tea made without the lemonade.

COSMOPOLITAN COCKTAIL

1 ½ oz. vodka
1 oz. Cointreau

1 oz. Cranberry juice
slice of lime or lemon

Combine liquid ingredients; mix in ice-filled cocktail shaker or pour over ice. Garnish with lemon or lime. Makes 1 serving.

Amy Polk

JAMES BOND MARTINI
(Adopted from Merchants Restaurant, NYC)
Per drink:

1 ½ oz. vodka
1 ½ oz. gin
½ oz. extra dry vermouth

½ oz. Lillet blanc
twist of lemon peel

Combine vodka, gin, vermouth and Lillet in a cocktail shaker partly filled with ice. Shake briefly. Strain into a chilled martini glass and garnish with lemon peel.

John Duncan

BLUEBERRY DAIQUIRI

(Reward your friends for picking those blueberries up at Lake Maratanza!)

Special Equipment: cocktail
   shaker
2 cups picked-over
   blueberries

⅓ cup water
¼ cup sugar, or to taste
4 oz. (½ cup) amber rum
¼ cup fresh lemon juice

Cook blueberries, water and sugar in a 1-1 ½ qt. sauce pan to a full boil, stirring, one minute. Transfer to a blender and blend until smooth. Force through a fine mesh sieve into a bowl, pressing hard on the solids, then discarding them. Set bowl in larger bowl full of ice and cold water and let stand, stirring occasionally, until cold, about 5 minutes. Fill a large cocktail shaker three-fourths full of ice cubes. Add blueberry syrup, rum and lemon juice and shake vigorously 5 seconds. Add sugar to taste, shaking to combine and strain into 4 (12 oz.) glasses filled with crushed ice.

John Duncan

FAKE EXPENSIVE BALSAMIC VINEGAR

1 bottle commercial
  balsamic vinegar
1 generous pinch brown
  sugar

1-2 cloves star anise
1 cinnamon stick

Combine all ingredients, boil down to ⅓ of original volume. Remove spices, decant.

Mary Kroul McAlpin

While driving on the Thruway one day I heard one of the chefs who talk on WAMC give this tidbit out. I contacted the station, but they had no record of it!

ORANGE PICO SALAD DRESSING

½ cup oil
¼ cup orange juice (or a
  couple Tbsp frozen
  concentrate)

2 Tbsp cider vinegar
1 ½ tsp sugar
dash of pepper

Mix together. Use this dressing with a salad of romaine lettuce, cucumber, mandarin oranges, red onion, sesame seeds and walnuts. This salad can also be augmented with tuna fish or pieces of chicken. Double the recipe and keep it around to use at a moments notice.

Anonymous

* * * * *

A messy kitchen is a happy kitchen and this kitchen is delirious.

Unknown

LIME HONEY MUSTARD GARLIC SALAD DRESSING

¼ cup freshly squeezed lime
   juice
2 Tbsp fat-free chicken broth
1 Tbsp honey
2 garlic cloves, minced

1 tsp Dijon mustard
2 Tbsp extra virgin olive oil
salt and freshly ground
   black pepper

    Whisk together lime juice, broth, honey, garlic and mustard. Slowly add the olive oil in a thin stream and whisk the dressing until it is blended. Season to taste with salt and pepper.

                               JoAnne Lindsley

    This dressing is perfect on all sorts of salads- light, tangy and low calorie.

RHUBARB CHUTNEY

1 pound rhubarb, diced
½ cup brown sugar, packed
¼ cup cider vinegar
¼ cup raisins

½ teaspoon grated lemon
   rind
½ teaspoon ground ginger
¼ teaspoon dry mustard
¼ teaspoon salt

    Combine all ingredients in heavy 2 qt. saucepan. Cook on high until bubbles form around edge. Reduce heat to low & simmer for 15 min.

                               F. Laun Maurer

CLARA'S PEACH CHUTNEY

2 29 oz cans cling peach
   slices
1 green pepper
1 large onion
½ cup light or dark seedless
   raisins
1 cup firmly packed brown
   sugar

1 ½ cups vinegar
¼ cup chopped preserved
   ginger
½ Tbsp salt
¼ Tbsp cloves
¼ Tbsp nutmeg
½ Tbsp cayenne pepper
¼ Tbsp black pepper

    Drain peaches, chop green pepper, chop onion and add remaining ingredients and simmer 1 to 1 ½ hours, until thickened. Makes about 1 quart.

                             M. A. P. Meisinger

RHUBARB/PRUNE JAM

3 pints diced rhubarb
1 box (12 oz.) prunes cut
 small

2 cups sugar (less will make
 more tart jam)
Grated rind of 1 orange

Cook in a small amount of water until the consistency is what you want

Dorothy Oakes

You may substitute raisins & lemons for prunes & orange

GRIT RESTAURANT MARINARA

3 tbs extra virgin olive oil
½ medium yellow onion,
 finely chopped
2 tbs minced fresh garlic
1 tbs finely chopped fresh
 parsley or 1 scant tsp dried
1 scant tbs fresh oregano or
 1 scant tsp dried
1 tbs finely chopped fresh
 basil or 1 scant tsp dried

1-½ tsp salt
1-½ tsp sugar
½ generous tsp freshly
 ground black pepper
⅔ c water
1 tsp freshly squeezed lemon
 juice
2 (28-ounce) cans crushed
 tomatoes

In a large, heavy-bottomed saucepan, heat oil over medium-high heat.

Add onions and garlic and sauté until onions are translucent and garlic is well sizzled, approximately 5 minutes.

Add remaining ingredients and stir often until mixture just begins to bubble.

Lower heat and simmer for 20 minutes, stirring frequently.

Yields approximately 8 cups.

Mara Lindsley Smith

* * * * *

My doctor told me to stop having intimate dinners for four. Unless there are three other people.

Orson Welles

TOMATO-BASIL-GARLIC OLIVE OIL PASTA SAUCE

¾ cup extra virgin olive oil
5 chopped garlic cloves
4 scallions
In winter: 1 can whole
  peeled tomatoes without
  juice or 10 large fresh
  cherry tomatoes cut in half

In summer: use 5 garden
  tomatoes quartered
2 cloves minced garlic
6 large basil leaves
sea salt (to taste)
grated parmesan cheese

(Use organic ingredients where possible.)
In a large skillet, saute chopped garlic in ¼ cup olive oil; add sliced scallions (cut ½ inch white, ¾-1 inch green); cook until soft; add remaining olive oil, tomatoes, minced garlic, chopped basil and sea salt; cook until fresh tomatoes are soft but still hold their shape; canned tomatoes will be softer. Serve over pasta or chicken; sprinkle with grated parmesan cheese.

Pat Peters
Dick Peters

MAKE-AHEAD TURKEY GRAVY

3 lb. turkey wings
2 medium onions,
  peeled/quartered
1 cup water
8 cups chicken broth

¾ cup chopped carrots
½ tsp dried thyme
¾ cup flour
2 Tbsp butter or margarine
½ Tbsp pepper

Heat oven to 400°F. Arrange wings in single layer in large roasting pan; scatter onions over top. Roast 1 ¼ hours until wings are browned. Put wings and onions in a large pot; add 6 cups broth along with carrot and thyme. Bring to a boil, reduce heat and simmer, uncovered for 1 ½ hours. Remove wings to a cutting board; when cool discard skin and reserve meat for another use (such as turkey salad). Strain broth into a 3-qt. saucepan, pressing vegetables to extract liquid. Discard vegetables; skim fat off broth. Whisk flour into remaining 2 cups broth and boil 3-4 minutes to thicken. Stir in butter and pepper. Serve immediately or refrigerate up to 1 week or freeze up to 3 months. Makes 8 cups.

Amy Polk

TEXAS BARBEQUE SAUCE

2 Tbsp brown sugar
1 Tbsp paprika
1 tsp salt
1 tsp dry mustard
¼ tsp chili powder
⅛ tsp cayenne pepper

2 Tbsp Worcestershire sauce
¼ cup vinegar
1 cup tomato juice
¼ cup catsup
½ cup water
¼- ½ cup chopped onion

Mix all ingredients together in a saucepan. Simmer for 15 minutes.

Joyce Stedner

HOT DOG TOPPING

1 lb. ground beef
1 cup chopped onion
1 cup ketchup
1 cup water
2 tsp sugar

1 tsp chili powder
⅛ tsp red pepper flakes
2 tsp regular mustard
1 tbsp cornstarch

Brown hamburger and onions. In a saucepan mix rest of ingredients. Mix in browned hamburger and onions and simmer 15 minutes. Serve on top of frankfurters.

Joyce Stedner

COFFEE GLAZE FOR BAKED HAM OR PORK

½ cup packed brown sugar
¼ cup maple syrup
2 Tbsp cider vinegar
1 Tbsp Worcestershire sauce

1 Tbsp instant coffee
 granules
1 Tbsp dry mustard

Stir together until coffee dissolves. Makes enough for a 7 lb. ham.

Amy Polk

* * * * *

Vegetables are a must on a diet. I suggest carrot cake, zucchini bread, and pumpkin pie.

Garfield

LAMB MARINADE

Equal parts soy sauce (low sodium is fine), dry white wine, olive oil
Add chopped fresh parsley usually ½ to 1 c

Minced fresh garlic 4-5 cloves (minced garlic in a jar works too)
Boned leg of lamb, or lamb chops

Mix all the ingredients in a jar and shake well, then marinate the lamb several hours, turn once or twice. Cook on the grill if possible, if not leave some marinade in the pan and cook the lamb in the oven.

Mary Ann Maurer

APPLESAUCE DELUXE

1 pkg. (3 oz.) raspberry jello
1 cup boiling water

1 ½ cups applesauce (15 oz. jar)
1 tsp lemon juice

Dissolve jello in boiling water, blend in applesauce and lemon. juice. Pour into glass bowl. Chill until firm. Makes about 2 ½ cups.

Audrey Keir

WONDERFUL JELLO

1 oz. package of Jello (strawberry or raspberry)
1 cup heavy cream
½ cup walnuts

1 cup strawberries or raspberries (fresh or frozen)

Prepare Jello and chill until mixture is starting to firm. Beat cream until stiff. Combine Jello and cream. Add nuts and berries.

Return mixture to refrigerator to complete chilling. Serves four.

Ann Fishman

GOOBER PEAS

(Peanuts)

raw (or green) peanuts

Peanuts should be green (raw), and kept refrigerated until you plan to cook them.

Rinse/float peanuts a minute or 2 in cold water, and once/twice in pot to remove any dirt. Remove any bad looking peanuts that float to top that you know you wouldn't want to eat. Drain water from pot and fill pot again with fresh water. Fill pot almost to the top (Usually, the pot boils over, but you can reduce the heat to med-high once they start boiling to keep that from happening). Be sure the peanuts float, otherwise the ones at the bottom that do not float may burn. Add ½ coffee cup (regular size) of salt, boil at high (perhaps med-high after boiling starts) for 1 ½ - 2 hours. Add water from time-to-time as needed so peanuts will always be floating. Stir once in a while so the ones at the top will get in the water. Taste after an hour or so to see if you want to add any more salt and to check texture. Remove pot from stove when finished cooking and immediately drain water so nuts don't soak up water. They can be eaten warm (immediately after being cooked), but don't let them sit and return to room temperature (they will dry-out). Any that aren't immediately eaten should be refrigerated.

Sarah Mack

POPCORN BALLS

⅔ cup dark Karo or sorghum
  syrup
2 cups sugar

½ cup whole milk or cream
3 large bowls of popcorn

Boil wet ingredients together to soft ball stage.

Pour over popcorn in large bowls which are no more than ⅔ full. Mix well and shape into balls.

**Angelena Abate, from my
Great-Grandmother**

HOMEMADE GRANOLA

1 cup powdered milk
1 cup unsalted sunflower
  seeds
1 cup sesame seeds
1 cup whole wheat flour
1 cup wheat germ
1 cup flax seeds (optional)

6 cups oats (not instant or
  quick cooking)
1 cup canola oil
1 cup honey
½- 1 cup dried fruits and
  nuts as desired (coconut,
  raisins, walnuts, almonds,
  cranberries)

Preheat oven at 275°F. Mix together dry ingredients and add oil and honey. Mix well and bake in a 9 x 13 pan for 30 minutes. Stir well and bake an additional 30 minutes. Remove from oven and stir. Add your favorite fruits and nuts. Enjoy!

Linda Rogers

* * * * *

I didn't fight my way to the top of the food chain to be a vegetarian.

Bumper Sticker

INDEX OF RECIPES

Breads & Pastries

Desserts

Miscellaneous

LIST OF CONTRIBUTORS

LIST OF CONTRIBUTORS

Cooking Hints & Tips

• Keep a recipe card upright by placing it in the tines of a fork and putting the fork handle in a glass.

• To keep a recipe book or card clean, place it under an upside-down glass pie plate. The curved bottom also magnifies the print.

• Use a photo album as a recipe book. Each time you cut a recipe out of a magazine, place it in one of the album's plastic sleeves.

• Glue an envelope to the inside of the front cover of your 'favorite' cookbook to hold new recipe cards or recipe clippings.

• Before you start baking or cooking, keep a plastic bag handy to slip over your hand when the phone rings.

• If butter is used in place of vegetable shortening, the amount of butter should be at least 1/4 more than the amount of shortening.

• It is best to cream butter by itself before adding the sugar.

• When a chocolate cake requires greasing and flouring the pans, try using cocoa instead of flour. When the cake is done, there will be no white flour residue on your cake and it adds flavor.

• Before measuring honey or other sticky ingredients, dip your spoon in oil.

• Put cold oil in a hot pan so the food won't stick.

• Add a pinch of baking soda to your frosting and the frosting will stay moist and prevent cracking.

• When you boil water, place a lid on the pot and the water will come to a boil in a shorter period of time– saving at least 10 minutes.

• To keep dough from sticking to your rolling pin, cover it with a clean stockinette.

• For shiny pie crusts, brush the crust lightly with milk.

• For sugary pie crusts, moisten the crust lightly with water or beaten egg whites, then sprinkle with sugar.

• Never salt food to be fried– it will draw moisture to the surface and cause spattering in the hot oil.

• Before heating the fat when deep fat frying, add one tablespoon white vinegar to minimize the amount of fat absorbed by the frying food. The food will taste less greasy.

• Sugar can be powdered by pounding it in a large mortar or rolling it on a paste-board with a rolling pin. It should be made very fine and always sifted.

Cooking Hints & Tips

• No more slow cooker mess—Before you start the recipe, place a turkey size browning bag in your cooker and put the ingredients inside the bag. After serving your dinner, just take the bag out and throw it away.

• Here's a neat casserole trick: When you are baking a covered casserole, keep your dish and oven neat by propping the lid open just a bit with a toothpick. This will prevent the casserole from bubbling over.

• Use double-thick paper towels to place over cooling rack to keep the rack from making imprints into the cake while cooling.

• Use one 3" pan instead of 2" layer pans for a higher cake—more cake less work. Slice lengthwise for layers.

• To make any home-made or boxed chocolate cake recipe moist and fluffier, add a spoonful of vinegar to the dry ingredients. You'll be amazed at the difference.

• Dip your icing spatula in hot water and dry with a paper towel. The heat from the water will melt the oil in the icing making it smoother.

• When you need a cake cooled and out of the pan quickly, place a cold wet towel or paper towels under the pan.

• Out of icing for your cup cakes? Just pop a marshmallow on top of each cup cake for about a minute before they come out of the oven. It will make a delicious, instant gooey frosting.

• Use dental floss to cut cakes, especially delicate, sticky ones that tend to adhere to a knife.

• Extend the shelf life of your home-made or store-bought cakes, by storing a half apple with them.

• Store a few lumps of sugar with your cheese to prevent it from molding.

• Apple sauce is a great fat substitute for low fat baking. Simply substitute half the fat in a recipe with an equal measure of applesauce.

• Disinfect your kitchen sponges by placing them in the microwave for 60 seconds.

• Peeling apples, pears and potatoes in cold, slightly salted water, will help keep them from turning brown.

• If soup tastes very salty, a raw piece of potato placed in the pot will absorb the salt.

• You can cut a meringue pie cleanly by coating both sides of a knife lightly with butter.

Cooking Hints & Tips

MICROWAVE SHORTCUTS

TOASTING NUTS–Place 1/2 cup of nuts in a 2-cup measure. Micro-cook, uncovered, on 100% power about 3 minutes or until toasted, stirring frequently.

BLANCHING ALMONDS– In a small nonmetal bowl, micro-cook 1 cup water, uncovered, on 100% power for 2-3 minutes or till boiling. Add 1/2 cup almonds to water. Micro-cook, uncovered, on 100% power for 1 1/2 minutes. Drain, rinse almonds with cold water. Slip off skins.

TOASTING COCONUT– Place flaked or shredded coconut in a 1-cup measure. Micro-cook, uncovered, on 100% power until light brown, stirring every 20 seconds. Allow 1 to 1 1/2 minutes for 1/4 cup and 1 1/2 to 2 minutes for 1/2 cup.

SOFTENING ICE CREAM– Micro-cook 1 pint solidly frozen ice cream, uncovered, on 100% power for about 15 seconds or until soft enough to serve.

PLUMPING DRIED FRUIT– In a 2-cup measure micro-cook 1 cup water, uncovered, on 100% power for 2-3 minutes or till boiling. Stir in 1/2 cup dried fruit. Let stand for 5-10 minutes.

SOFTENING BUTTER OR MARGARINE– Place unwrapped butter or margarine in a micro-safe dish. Micro-cook, uncovered, on 10% power, allowing about 25-30 seconds for 2 tablespoons or about 40 seconds for 1/4 cup butter or margarine.

SOFTENING CREAM CHEESE– Place an unwrapped 3-ounce package of cream cheese in a small micro-safe bowl. Micro-cook, uncovered on 30% power about 1 minute or until soft.

MELTING CHOCOLATE PIECES– In a glass measure micro-cook chocolate pieces, uncovered, on 100% power until melted, stirring once. Allow 1-1/2 minutes for 3 oz. or 1-1/2 to 2 minutes for a 6-ounce package.

MELTING CARAMEL– Place unwrapped caramel in a glass measure. Micro-cook, on 100% power stirring once. Allow 45 seconds to 1 minute for 14 caramels (about 1/2 cup) or 1 to 1 1/2 minutes for 28 (about a cup).

PEELING TOMATOES– In a 2-cup measure micro-cook 1 cup water, uncovered, on 100% power for 2-3 minutes or until boiling. Spear 1 tomato with a long tined fork. Submerge into hot water; hold about 12 seconds. Place tomato under cold water, slip off skin.

Cooking & Food Terms

AL DENTÉ– Describes foods, especially pasta, cooked only until soft enough to eat, but not over-done. The Italian translation is "to the teeth."

ADJUST SEASONING– To taste the dish before serving to determine the need for salt, herbs, or other seasonings.

BLACKEN– A method of cooking in which meat or fish is seasoned with a spicy mixture then fried in a hot skillet until blackened on both sides.

BLANCH– Blanching is a process in which food is briefly plunged in boiling water for a moment, then immediately transferred to ice water to stop the cooking process. Blanching tomatoes or peaches for about 20 sec. makes them easier to peel.

BRAISE– Braising involves cooking a food in a little fat to brown, usually on the stove top then covering and cooking slowly until done. This is particularly suited to less tender cuts of meat.

BROIL– To cook food directly under or over heat source, usually in the oven under the top broiling element or on the grill.

BROWN– To cook food quickly at a moderately high heat to brown the surface. May be done on the stove top or under the broiler in the oven.

BUTTERFLY– To cut a food down the center, but not quite through, leaving both halves attached, The food is then spread to resemble a butterfly.

CHUNKS– Usually bite-size pieces, about 1-inch or larger.

CLARIFIED BUTTER– Unsalted butter which has been melted and skimmed of milk solids.

CUBE– To cut into cubes, about 1/2 to 1-inch. Cube may also mean to tenderize meat with a tenderizing mallet or utensil which makes "cubes" imprints.

CURE– To preserve food, usually meat or fish, by pickling, smoking, drying, salting, or storing in a brine.

CUT IN– To incorporate solid fat into dry ingredients using a pastry blender or knives.

DASH– Less than 1/8 teaspoon.

DEEP-FAT FRY– To cook in hot fat which is deep enough to completely cover the food.

DEGLAZE– To add liquid to the pan in which meat or other food was cooked. The liquid, usually broth or wine, is heated to loosen the browned bits left in the pan, and is often used as a base for sauce or gravy.

Cooking & Food Terms

DEGREASE– To remove melted fat from the surface of liquid, usually by skimming with a spoon, refrigerating to solidify the fat, or by using a cup or pitcher designed to separate the fat from the liquid.

DEHYDRATE– To remove moisture from food by drying it slowly in the oven or in an electric or manual dehydrator.

DEVEIN– To remove the vein from the back of shrimp or to remove the interior ribs from peppers.

DICE– To cut food into cubes about 1/8 to 3/4 inch in size.

DOLLOP– A spoonful of soft food, such as mashed potatoes or whipped cream. It may also mean a dash or "splash" of soda water, water, or other liquid if referring to liquid.

DOT– To scatter bits of an ingredient (usually butter) evenly over the surface of another food.

DOUGH– A mixture of flour, liquid, and other ingredients. Dough is too thick to pour but thick enough to roll out or work with hands.

DREDGE– To coat food with a dry mixture (usually seasoned flour or crumbs), either by sprinkling, rolling, or shaking the food in a bag with the flour or other ingredients.

DRIPPINGS– The juices or liquefied fats left in a pan after cooking meat or other food.

DRIZZLE– To pour a thin mixture, such as melted butter or thin icing, over food in a very fine stream.

DUMPLING– Large or small amounts of dough usually dropped into a liquid mixture such as broth, stew, or fruit. (2) A fruit or fruit mixture encased in sweet dough and baked.

EGG WASH– Egg yolk or white mixed with a small amount of water or liquid then brushed over baked goods to give color and sheen.

EN CROUTE– Food baked in a crust.

EVAPORATED MILK– A canned, unsweetened milk is homogenized milk from which 60% of the water has been re-moved. Whole evaporated milk contains at least 7.9 percent butterfat, while the skim version contains 1/2 percent or less.

EXTRACT– Concentrated flavors from various foods, usually derived from distillation or evaporation. Extracts, also called essences, may be solid or liquid.

Cooking & Food Terms

FILLET– A boneless piece of meat or fish.

FLAKE– To use a fork or other utensil to break off pieces or layers of food.

FLANK STEAK– A long, fibrous cut of beef which comes from an animal's lower hindquarters. Flank steak is usually tenderized by marinating, then boiled or grilled and cut thinly across the grain.

FLOUR– To lightly sprinkle or coat with flour.

FLUTE– To press a scalloped or decorative design into the edge of a pie crust.

FOLD– To incorporate a light mixture with a heavy mixture, such as beaten egg whites into batter or custard. The lighter mixture is placed on the heavier mixture, and a spatula is used to gently cut down and through the lighter mixture of the bottom of the bowl then up again. This procedure gently turns the mixtures over on top of each other, and is repeated until the two mixtures are combined.

FRENCH FRY– To deep-fry food, such as strips of potatoes.

FRICASSEE– To cook or stew pieces of sauteed meat in a sauce, usually with vegetables. Wine is often used as a flavoring.

FRIZZLE– To fry thin slices of meat or other food until the edges curl.

FROST– To apply sugar, frosting, glaze, or icing to fruit, cake, or other food.

FRY– To cook food in a fat over moderate to high heat.

GARNISH– To decorate food or the dish on which food is served.

GLAZE– A thin, glossy coating applied to the surface of a food. A glaze may also add flavor.

GRATE– To cut food into small shreds or particles, usually with a food grater.

GRATIN DISH– A shallow baking dish or pan, usually round or oval in shape.

GREASE– To spread fat (or non-stick cooking spray) on a cooking utensil or pan to prevent food from sticking. To grease and flour means to grease the pan then dust with flour. The flour is sprinkled into the greased pan then the pan is shaken to distribute evenly before inverting and discarding the excess.

GRILL– To cook on a rack directly over hot coals or other heat source.

Cooking & Food Terms

GRIND– To reduce food to small particles, as in ground coffee, ground beef, or ground spices. A variety of instruments may be used, including mortar and pestle, meat grinder, pepper mills, and food processor.

HALF AND HALF– A mixture of half cream, half milk. The fat content is between 10 and 12 percent.

INFUSE– To immerse tea, herbs, or other flavoring ingredients in a hot liquid in order to extract flavor.

JELL– To congeal, often with the addition of gelatin.

JIGGER– A liquid measure equal to 1-1/2 fluid ounces.

JULIENNE– To cut food into thin, matchstick strips. Julienne strips are usually about 1/8 inch thick, but the length varies.

KNEAD– A technique used to mix and work dough, usually using the hands. Dough is pressed with the heels of the hands, while stretching it out, then folded over itself.

LARD– Rendered and clarified pork fat. As a verb, to lard is to insert strips of fat into uncooked lean meat (such as venison) to tenderize and add flavor.

LEAVENER– An ingredient or agent used to lighten the texture and increase volume in baked goods. Baking powder, baking soda, and yeast are common leaveners.

LIQUEUR– Sweet alcoholic drink usually served after a meal. Liqueurs are usually flavored with aromatic ingredients such as nuts, fruits, flowers, or spices, and are frequently used in baked desserts and dessert sauces.

MARINATE– To let food soak in a seasoned liquid in order to flavor and tenderize.

MASH– To crush a food until smooth and evenly textured.

MEDALLION– A small, round cut of meat, usually pork, veal, or beef.

MELT– Heating a food (such as shortening, butter, or chocolate) until it becomes liquid.

MINCE– To chop food into small pieces, usually 1/8 inch or less.

MIX– To blend ingredients.

MOLD– To form a food into a shape by hand, or by placing or pouring into a decorative container (or mold) then refrigerating or cooking until firm enough to hold its shape.

MOUSSE– A sweet or savory dish, made with egg whites or whipped cream to give the light, airy texture.

Cooking & Food Terms

MULL– To flavor a beverage, such as cider or wine, by heating it with spices or other flavorings.

PARBOIL– To boil a food briefly, until partially done. A food might be parboiled before adding it to faster-cooking ingredients to insure all ingredients are evenly cooked.

PARE– To cut the skin from a food, usually with a short knife called a paring knife.

PASTEURIZE– To kill bacteria by heating liquids to moderately high temperatures only briefly. French scientist Louis Pasteur discovered the solution while he was researching the cause of beer and wine spoilage.

PASTRY BAG– A cone-shaped bag with openings at both ends. Food is placed into the large opening then squeezed out the small opening which may be fitted with a decorator tip. It has a variety of uses, including decorating cakes and cookies, forming pastries, or piping decorative edging. Bags may be made of cloth, plastic, or other materials.

PASTRY BLENDER– A kitchen utensil with several u-shaped wires attached to a handle. It's used to cut solid fat (like shortening or butter) into flour and other dry ingredients in order to evenly distribute the fat particles.

PASTRY BRUSH– A brush used to apply glaze or egg wash to breads and other baked goods either before or after baking.

PASTRY WHEEL– A utensil with a cutting wheel attached to a handle. It's used to mark and cut rolled-out dough, and may have a plain or decorative edge.

PIPE– To squeeze icing or other soft food through a pastry bag to make a design or decorative edible edging.

PIQUANT– A term which generally means tangy flavor.

PIT– To remove the seed or stone of a fruit or berry.

POACH– To cook in liquid at or just below the boiling point. For eggs, meat, or fish, the liquid is usually water or a seasoned stock; fruit is generally poached in a sugar syrup.

PREHEAT– To allow the oven or pan to get to a specified temperature before adding the food to be cooked.

PRESERVE– To prepare foods for long storage. Some ways to preserve foods are drying, freezing, canning, curing, pickling, and smoking.

PRICK– To make small holes in the surface of a food, usually using the tines of a fork. Pie crust is usually pricked.

Cooking & Food Terms

PULVERIZE– To reduce to a powder or dust by pounding, crushing or grinding.

PUREE– To blend, process, sieve, or mash a food until it's very smooth and has the consistency of baby food.

REDUCE– To boil a liquid until a portion of it has evaporated. Reducing intensifies the flavor and results in a thicker liquid.

RENDER– To extract the fat from meat by cooking over low heat. Rendered fat is strained of meat particles after cooking.

ROAST– To cook food in an open pan in the oven, with no added liquid.

ROLLING BOIL– A very fast boil that doesn't slow when stirred.

SAUTÉ– To cook quickly in a pan on top of the stove until the food is browned.

SCORE– To cut shallow slashes unto ham or other food, to allow excess fat to drain, or to help tenderize.

SEAR– To brown meat quickly over high heat. Meat may be seared under a broiler or in a skillet on top of the stove.

SHRED– To cut food into narrow strips. A grater or food processor may be used to shred.

SIFT– To pass dry ingredients through a mesh sifter. Incorporates air, which makes food lighter.

SIMMER– To cook liquid at about 185° or just below boil. Tiny bubbles just beginning to break the surface.

SKIM– To remove a substance from the surface of a liquid.

SLIVER– To cut a food into thin strips or pieces.

STEEP– To soak, in order to extract flavor or soften.

STRAIN– To pour liquid through a strainer or colander to remove solid particles.

THICKEN– To make liquid more thick by reducing or adding a roux, starch, or eggs.

THIN– To dilute a mixture by adding more liquid.

TRUSS– To hold food together so it will retain its shape. Poultry and some roasts are often tied with twine or held together with skewers.

WATERBATH– To place a container of food in a large pan of warm water, which surrounds the food with heat.

WHIP– To beat ingredients with a whisk, or other utensil, which incorporates air into a mixture and changes the texture.

Ingredient Substitutions

INGREDIENT	AMOUNT	SUBSTITUTE
Allspice	1 tsp.	• 1/2 tsp. cinnamon and 1/2 tsp. ground cloves
Apple Pie Spice	1 tsp.	• 1/2 tsp. cinnamon, 1/4 tsp. nutmeg, and 1/8 tsp. cardamom
Arrowroot	1 1/2 tsp.	• 1 tsp flour • 1 1/2 tsp. cornstarch
Baking Powder	1 tsp.	• 1/3 tsp. baking soda and 1/2 tsp. cream of tartar • 1/4 tsp. baking soda and 1/2 cup sour milk or buttermilk (Decrease liquid called for in recipe by 1/2 cup.)
Bay Leaf	1 whole	• 1/8 to 1/4 tsp., crushed
Bread	1 slice dry 1 slice soft	• 1/3 cup dry bread crumbs • 3/4 cup bread crumbs
Broth, Beef or Chicken	1 cup	• 1 bouillon cube dissolved in 1 cup boiling water • 1 envelope powdered broth base dissolved in 1 cup boiling water • 1 1/2 tsp. powdered broth base dissolved in 1 cup boiling water
Butter	1 cup	• 7/8 to 1 cup hydrogenated fat and 1/2 tsp. salt • 7/8 cup lard plus 1/2 tsp. salt • 1 cup margarine
Buttermilk (sour milk)	1 cup	• 1 cup plain yogurt • 1 cup whole or skim milk plus 1 Tbsp. lemon juice or white vinegar • 1 cup milk plus 1 3/4 tsp. cream of tartar
Chili Sauce	1 cup	• 1 cup catsup, 1/4 tsp. cinnamon, dashes of ground cloves and allspice

Ingredient Substitutions

INGREDIENT	AMOUNT	SUBSTITUTE
Chives, Finely Chopped	2 tsp.	• 2 tsp. green onion tops finely chopped
Chocolate, Chips Semisweet	1 oz.	• 1 oz. sweet cooking chocolate
Chocolate, Semisweet	1 2/3 oz. 6 oz. pkg.	• 1 oz. unsweetened chocolate plus 4 tsp. sugar • 1 cup
Chocolate, Unsweetened	1 oz. sq.	• 3 Tbsp. cocoa plus 1 Tbsp. fat
Cocoa	1/4 cup or 4 Tbsp.	• 1 oz. sq. unsweetened chocolate (decrease fat called for in recipe by 1/2 Tbsp.)
Coconut Cream	1 cup	• 1 cup whipping cream
Coconut Milk	1 cup	• 1 cup whole or 2% milk
Corn	1 doz. ears	• 2 1/2 cups cooked
Cornmeal, Self-rising	1 cup	• 7/8 cup plain, 1 1/2 Tbsp. baking powder, and 1/2 tsp. salt
Corn Syrup, Dark	1 cup	• 3/4 cup light corn syrup and 1/4 cup light molasses
Cornstarch (for thickening)	1 Tbsp.	• 2 Tbsp. all purpose flour • 2 Tbsp. granular tapioca
Cracker Crumbs	3/4 cup	• 1 cup dry bread crumbs
Cream, Heavy (36% to 40% fat)	1 cup	• 3/4 cup milk and 1/3 cup butter or margarine (for use in cooking or baking)

Ingredient Substitutions

INGREDIENT	AMOUNT	SUBSTITUTE
Cream, Light (18% to 20% fat)	1 cup	• 3/4 cup milk and 3 Tbsp. butter or margarine (for use in cooking or baking) • 1 cup evaporated milk, undiluted
Cream, Whipped	2 tsp.	• Chill a 13 oz-can of evaporated milk until ice crystals form. Add 1 tsp. lemon juice. Whip until stiff
Dates	1 lb.	• 2 1/2 cups pitted
Dill Plant, Fresh or Dried	3 heads	• 1 Tbsp. dill seed
Egg, Whole, Uncooked	1 large (3 Tbsp.)	• 3 Tbsp. and 1 tsp. thawed frozen egg • 2 1/2 Tbsp. sifted, dry whole egg powder and 2 1/2 Tbsp. lukewarm water • 2 yolks 1 Tbsp. water (in cookies) • 2 yolks (in custard, cream fillings, and similar mixture) • 2 whites as a thickening agent
Eggs, Uncooked	1 cup = ▸	• 5 large • 6 medium
Egg White	1 large (2 Tbsp.)	• 2 Tbsp. sifted, dry egg white powder, and 2 Tbsp. lukewarm water
	1 cup = ▸	• 8 large egg whites
Egg Yolk (1 1/2 Tbsp.)	1 yolk	• 3 1/2 Tbsp. thawed frozen egg yolk • 2 Tbsp. sifted, dry egg yolk
	1 cup = ▸	• 12 large egg yolks
Fines Herbes	1/3 cup	• 3 Tbsp. parsley flakes, 2 tsp. dried chervil, 2 tsp. dried chives, 1 tsp. dried tarragon

Ingredient Substitutions

INGREDIENT	AMOUNT	SUBSTITUTE
Flour, All-purpose (for thickening)	1 Tbsp.	• 1 1/2 tsp. cornstarch, arrowroot starch, potato starch, or rice starch • 1 tsp. waxy rice flour • 1 1/2 Tbsp. whole wheat flour • 1 tsp. quick-cooking tapioca
Flour, All-purpose	1 cup sifted	• 1 cup and 2 Tbsp. cake flour • 1 cup rolled oats, crushed
	1 lb.	• 4 cups sifted • 3 1/3 cups unsifted
Flour, Cake	1 lb.	• 4 3/4 cups
	1 cup sifted	• 1 cup minus 2 Tbsp. sifted all-purpose flour
Flour, Self-rising	1 cup	• 1 cup minus 2 tsp. all-purpose flour, 1 1/2 tsp. baking powder, and 1/2 tsp. salt

NOTE: Substitutes for white flours added to most baked goods will result in a reduced volume and a heavier product. Substitute no more than 1/4 of white flour in a cake to ensure success. In other recipes, you can substitute whole wheat flour for 1/4 to 1/2 white flour.

INGREDIENT	AMOUNT	SUBSTITUTE
Garlic	1 clove	• 1/8 tsp. garlic powder
Gelatin, Flavored	3 oz.	• 1 Tbsp. plain gelatin and 2 cups of fruit juice
Honey	1 cup	• 1 1/4 cup sugar and 1/4 cup water
Ketchup	1 cup	• 1 cup tomato sauce, 1/4 cup brown sugar, and 2 Tbsp. vinegar (for use in cooking)
Lemon Juice	1 tsp.	• 1/2 tsp. vinegar
Lemon Peel, Dried	1 tsp.	• 1 to 2 tsp. grated fresh lemon peel • 1/2 tsp. lemon extract

Ingredient Substitutions

INGREDIENT	AMOUNT	SUBSTITUTE
Marshmallows, Miniature	1 cup	• 8-10 regular
Mayonnaise	1 cup	• 1/2 cup yogurt and 1/2 cup mayonnaise • 1 cup of sour cream
Milk, Buttermilk	1 cup	• 1 cup sweet milk and 1 3/4 tsp. cream of tartar
Milk, Skim	1 cup	• 1/2 cup evaporated milk and 1/2 cup water
Milk, Sweetened	1 can (about 1 1/3 cups)	• Heat the following ingredients until sugar and butter are dissolved: 1/3 cup plus 2 tsp. evaporated milk, 1 cup sugar, and 3 Tbsp. butter or margarine
Milk, Whole	1 cup	• 1 cup reconstituted non-fat dry milk (Add 2 Tbsp. butter or margarine, if desired.) • 1/2 cup evaporated milk and 1/2 cup water
Mustard, Dry	1 tsp.	• 1 Tbsp. prepared mustard
Onion, Fresh	1 small	• Rehydrate 1 Tbsp. instant minced onion
Onion, Powdered	1 Tbsp.	• 1 medium onion • 4 Tbsp. fresh chopped
Onion	1 lb.	• 3 large onions • 2 to 2 1/2 cups chopped
Orange Peel, Dried	1 Tbsp.	• 2 to 3 Tbsp. grated orange peel
Parsley, Dried	1 tsp.	• 3 tsp. fresh parsley, chopped

Ingredient Substitutions

INGREDIENT	AMOUNT	SUBSTITUTE
Pumpkin Pie Spice	1 tsp.	• 1/2 tsp. cinnamon, 1/4 tsp. ginger, 1/8 tsp. allspice, and 1/8 tsp. nutmeg
Shortening, Melted	1 cup	• 1 cup cooking oil (Substitute only if recipe calls for melted shortening)
Shortening, Solid (used in baking)	1 cup	• 1 1/8 cups butter (Decrease salt called for in recipe by 1/2 tsp.)
Sour Cream, Cultured	1 cup	• 1 cup plain yogurt • 3/4 cup milk, 3/4 tsp. lemon juice, and 1/3 cup butter or margarine
Sugar, Brown	1 cup firmly packed	• 1 cup granulated sugar
	1 lb. = ▸	• 2 1/4 cups firmly packed
Sugar, Granulated	1 lb. = ▸	• 2 1/4 cups
Sugar, Powdered	1 lb. = ▸	• 2 3/4 cups
Sugar, Granulated	1 tsp.	• 1/8 tsp. noncaloric sweetener solution or follow manufacturer's directions
Sugar, Granulated	1 cup	• 1 1/2 cups corn syrup (Decrease liquid called for in recipe by 1/4 cup.) • 1 cup of powdered sugar • 1 cup, brown sugar, firmly packed • 3/4 cup honey (Decrease liquid called for in recipe by 1/4 cup; for each cup of honey in baked goods, add 1/2 tsp. soda.)
Tomato Juice	1 cup	• 1 cup tomato sauce and 1/2 cup water
Yogurt, Plain	1 cup	• 1 cup of buttermilk • 1 cup of sour cream

Yields & Equivalents

FOOD	YOUR RECIPE STATES	YOU WILL NEED
Apples	▸ 1 cup sliced or chopped ▸ 1 lb.	◂ 1 medium (6 oz.) ◂ 3 medium
Apricots, Dried Halves	1 cup	5 oz.
Asparagus	16 to 20 stalks	1 lb.
Bacon	1/2 cup crumbled	8 slices, crisply cooked
Bananas	▸ 1 cup sliced ▸ 1 cup mashed	◂ 1 medium or 2 small ◂ 2 medium
Beans	5 to 6 cups cooked	1 lb. dried (2 1/4 cups)
Beans, Green or Wax	3 cups 1-inch pieces	1 lb.
Bread, White	▸ 12 slices (1/2 inch) ▸ 1 cup soft ▸ 1 cup dry	◂ 1-lb loaf ◂ 1 1/2 slices ◂ 4 to 5 slices, oven-dried
Broccoli	2 cups flowerets, 1-inch pieces or chopped	6 oz.
Butter	1/2 cup	1 stick
Cabbage, Green Slaw (bag)	▸ 1 medium head ▸ 4 cups shredded	◂ 1 1/2 lb. ◂ 1 lb.
Carrots	▸ 1 medium ▸ 1 cup shredded ▸ 1 cup 1/4-inch slices	◂ 7 inches ◂ 1 1/2 medium ◂ 2 medium
Cauliflower	▸ 1 medium head ▸ 3 cups flowerets	◂ 2 lb. (with leaves) ◂ 1 lb.
Celery	▸ 1 medium bunch ▸ 1 cup thinly sliced or chopped	◂ 2 lb. (11 inches) ◂ 2 medium stalks

Yields & Equivalents

FOOD	YOUR RECIPE STATES	YOU WILL NEED
Cheese, Hard Cottage Cream	▸ 1 cup ▸ 2 cups ▸ 1 cup	◂ 4 oz. ◂ 16 oz. ◂ 8 oz.
Corn, Sweet	▸ 1 medium ear ▸ 1 cup kernels	◂ 8 oz. ◂ 2 medium ears
Cream, Sour Whipping (heavy)	▸ 1 cup ▸ 1 cup (2 cups whipped)	◂ 8 oz. ◂ 1/2 pt.
Crumbs, Finely Crushed Chocolate Wafer Cookie Graham Cracker Saltine Cracker Vanilla Wafer	 ▸ 1 1/2 cups ▸ 1 1/2 cups ▸ 1 cup ▸ 1 1/2 cups	 ◂ 27 cookies ◂ 21 squares ◂ 29 squares ◂ 38 cookies
Eggs, Large Whole	▸ 1 cup ▸ 1 egg	◂ 4 large ◂ 1/4 cup fat free egg product
Flour	3 1/2 cups	1 lb.
Garlic	1/2 tsp. finely chopped	1 medium clove
Lemons or Limes	▸ 1 1/2 to 3 tsp. grated peel ▸ 2 to 3 Tbsp. juice	◂ 1 medium ◂ 1 medium
Meat, Cooked Beef, Pork and Poultry	1 cup chopped or bite-size pieces	6 oz.
Mushrooms, Fresh Canned	▸ 6 cups sliced ▸ 2 1/2 cups chopped 4-oz. can sliced, drained	◂ 1 lb. ◂ 8 oz. ◂ 2/3 cup fresh, sliced and cooked (5 oz. uncooked)

Yields & Equivalents

FOOD	YOUR RECIPE STATES	YOU WILL NEED
Nuts, (without shells) Chopped, Sliced or Slivered	▶ 1 cup	◀ 4 oz.
Whole or Halves	▶ 3 to 4 cups	◀ 1 lb.
Olives, Pimiento-stuffed Ripe, Pitted	▶ 1 cup sliced ▶ 1 cup sliced	◀ 24 large or 36 small ◀ 32 medium
Oranges	▶ 1 Tbsp. grated peel ▶ 1/3 to 1/2 cup juice	◀ 1 medium ◀ 1 medium
Pasta, Macaroni Noodles, egg Spaghetti	▶ 4 cups cooked ▶ 4 cups cooked ▶ 4 cups cooked	◀ 2 cups uncooked (6-7 oz.) ◀ 4 to 5 cups uncooked (7 oz.) ◀ 7 to 8 oz. uncooked
Peppers, Bell	▶ 1/2 cup chopped ▶ 1 cup chopped ▶ 1 1/2 cups chopped	◀ 1 small ◀ 1 medium ◀ 1 large
Rice, Brown Parboiled (converted) Precooked White Instant Regular Long Grain Wild	▶ 4 cups cooked ▶ 3 to 4 cups cooked ▶ 2 cups cooked ▶ 3 cups cooked ▶ 3 cups cooked	◀ 1 cup uncooked ◀ 1 cup uncooked ◀ 1 cup uncooked ◀ 1 cup uncooked ◀ 1 cup uncooked
Shrimp (uncooked, with shells) Jumbo Large Medium Small	▶ 1 lb. ▶ 1 lb. ▶ 1 lb. ▶ 1 lb.	◀ 21 to 25 count ◀ 31 to 35 count ◀ 41 to 45 count ◀ 51 to 60 count
Cooked (without shells)	▶ 1 lb.	◀ 1 1/3 lb. uncooked (with shells)

Yields & Equivalents

TEASPOONS	TEASPOONS	CUPS	FLUID OZ.	MILLI-LITERS	OTHER
1/4 teaspoon				1 ml.	
1/2 teaspoon				2 ml.	
3/4 teaspoon	1/4 tablespoon			4 ml.	
1 teaspoon	1/3 tablespoon			5 ml.	
3 teaspoons	1 tablespoon	1/16 cup	1/2 oz.	15 ml.	
6 teaspoons	2 tablespoons	1/8 cup	1 oz.	30 ml.	
			1 1/2 oz.	44 ml.	1 jigger
12 teaspoons	4 tablespoons	1/4 cup	2 oz.	60 ml.	
16 teaspoons	5 1/3 tablespoons	1/3 cup	2 1/2 oz.	75 ml.	
18 teaspoons	6 tablespoons	3/8 cup	3 oz.	90 ml.	
24 teaspoons	8 tablespoons	1/2 cup	4 oz.	125 ml.	1/4 pint
32 teaspoons	10 2/3 tablespoons	2/3 cup	5 oz.	150 ml.	
36 teaspoons	12 tablespoons	3/4 cup	6 oz.	175 ml.	
48 teaspoons	16 tablespoons	1 cup	8 oz.	237 ml.	1/2 pint
		1 1/2 cups	12 oz.	355 ml.	
		2 cups	16 oz.	473 ml.	1 pint
		3 cups	24 oz.	710 ml.	1 1/2 pints
			25.6 oz.	757 ml.	1 fifth
		4 cups	32 oz.	946 ml.	1 quart or 1 liter
		8 cups	64 oz.		2 quarts
		16 cups	128 oz.		1 gallon

Dash or Pinch– Less than 1/8 tsp.

Firmly Packed– Tightly pressed ingredients in measuring cup.

Lightly Packed– Lightly pressed ingredients in measuring cup.

Even / Level– Precise measure. Discard any ingredients that rise above the rim of the measuring cup.

Rounded– Allow ingredients to pile above the rim measuring cup into a nice round shape.

Heaping– Pile as much of the ingredient on top of the measure as it can hold.

Sifted– Sift before measuring to ensure ingredient is not compacted.

General Oven Chart

Very Slow Oven	250 to 300° F.
Slow Oven	300 to 325° F.
Moderate Oven	325 to 375° F.
Medium Hot Oven	375 to 400° F.
Hot Oven	400 to 450° F.
Very Hot Oven	450 to 500° F

BREADS

Baking Powder Biscuits	400° F.	12 - 15 min.
Muffins	400° - 425° F.	25 - 35 min.
Quick Breads	350° - 375° F.	25 - 35 min.
Yeast Breads	375° - 400° F.	45 - 60 min.
Yeast Rolls	400° F.	15 - 20 min.

CAKES

Butter Loaf Cakes	350° F.	45 - 60 min.
Butter Layer Cakes	350° - 375° F.	25 - 35 min.
Cup Cakes	375° F.	20 - 23 min.
Chiffon Cakes	325° F.	60 min.
Sponge Cakes	325° F.	60 min.
Angel Food Cakes	325° F.	60 min.

COOKIES

Bar Cookies	350° F.	25 - 30 min.
Drop Cookies	350° - 375° F.	18 - 25 min.
Rolled Refrigerator Cookies	350° - 400° F.	8 - 12 min.

PASTRY

Meringue	350° F.	12 - 20 min.
Pie Shells	450° F.	12 - 15 min.
Filled Pies	450° F. lower to 350° F.	8 - 12 min.

NOTES: These are just general temperatures and times, always use what is specified in the recipe.

Modern oven thermostats are adjustable, so it is necessary to periodically check the ACTUAL oven temperature with an accurate thermometer designed for the purpose and adjust the dial, or have your serviceman perform this service at least once a year.

Always follow HIGH ALTITUDE directions, temperature settings and times when appropriate to your locale.

Meats
Seasonings & Marinades

FLAVORING CHART

MEAT	SEASONINGS			
Beef	rosemary sage garlic dill	mushrooms dry mustard shallots paprika	chili peppers peppercorns berries tomatoes	beer red wine balsamic vinegar
Chicken or Turkey	lemon ginger tarragon sage	thyme oregano dill peppers	garlic apple cider dry mustard fruit juices	paprika red wine white wine
Fish	cilantro bay leaf basil fennel	lemon lime dill saffron	black pepper garlic sweet peppers tarragon	rosemary herbed vinegar
Lamb	garlic curry mint lemon	rosemary thyme sage ginger	saffron mustard seed	
Pork	apples garlic ginger lemon	cloves rosemary orange zest lemon zest	coriander unsweetened preserves dried fruits	Madeira or port wine
Veal	ginger oregano mustard marjoram	shallots mushrooms orange lemon	Marsala wine garlic thyme	
Veg.	garlic lemon dill vinegar	nuts parsley mint rosemary	basil allspice sweet peppers pepper flakes	marjoram chervil chives nutmeg

TIP: For added flavor, blend garlic and herbs (fresh or dried) into a dish ahead of time. At the last minute of cooking time, toss in. This gives an extra dimension in taste.

Meats
Doneness Chart

DESCRIPTION	DEGREES FAHRENHEIT
Ground Meat & Mixtures	
Turkey, Chicken	165° F.
Veal, Beef, Lamb, Pork	160° F.
Fresh Beef	
Medium Rare	145° F.
Medium	160° F.
Well Done	170° F.
Fresh Veal	
Medium Rare	145° F.
Medium	160° F.
Well Done	170° F.
Fresh Lamb	
Medium Rare	145° F.
Medium	160° F.
Well Done	170° F.
Pork	
Well Done	170° F.
Poultry	
Chicken, Whole	180° F.
Turkey, Whole	180° F.
Poultry Breasts, Roasted	170° F.
Poultry Thighs, Wings	180° F.
Duck & Goose	180° F.
Seafood	
Fin Fish	Cook until opaque and flakes easily.
Shrimp, Lobster, Crab	Shell should turn red. Flesh pearly opaque.
Scallops	Flesh should turn milky white or opaque and firm.
Clams, Mussels, Oysters	Cook until shells open. Discard any unopened.

Candy Making Chart

Important tips to remember when making candy:

1. Dissolve sugar completely to keep large crystals from forming; wash down the sides of the saucepan by placing a cover over the saucepan for about 2-3 minutes.

2. Heavy, flat bottom saucepans will prevent candies from scorching.

3. A candy thermometer is essential for proper temperature.

4. Cool fudges to lukewarm before beating or shaping.

5. Butter, not margarine, should be used in most candy recipes to ensure the best textures and results.

Thread	begins at 230°	The syrup will make a 2" thread when dropped from a spoon.
Soft Ball	begins at 234°	A small amount of syrup dropped into chilled water forms a ball, but flattens when picked up with fingers.
Firm Ball	begins at 244°	The ball will hold its shape and flatten only when pressed.
Hard Ball	begins at 250°	The ball is more rigid but still pliable.
Soft Crack	begins at 270°	When a small amount of syrup is dropped into chilled water it will separate into threads which will bend when picked up.
Hard Crack	begins at 300°	The syrup separates into threads that are hard and brittle.
Caramelized	Sugar 310° to 338°	Between these temperatures the syrup will turn dark golden, but will turn black at 350°.

Herbs & Spices

ALLSPICE– Usually used in ground form, allspice has a flavor like a combination of cinnamon, nutmeg, and cloves. Allspice is used in both savory and sweet dishes.

ANISE SEED– Related to parsley, this spice has a mildly sweet licorice flavor.

BASIL– Most people are accustomed to using fresh basil in their favorite Italian dishes, but this licorice-like herb is equally at home in Thai coconut curry or a Provencal pistou. Dried basil tastes completely different from fresh, so if you want to add a shot of basil flavor try blending basil with olive oil and storing cubes in the freezer.

BAY LEAF– A pungent flavor. Available as whole leaf. Good in vegetable and fish soups, tomato sauces and juice. Remove before serving.

CARAWAY– Their slightly anise flavor works particularly well with rye breads as well with the kind of sweet and sour dishes favored in Central Europe such as pork and apples or braised red cabbage.

CARDAMOM– Whole cardamom pods can appear in pilaf rice, curries, or Scandinavian baked goods. Ground cardamom loses its flavor.

CAYENNE PEPPER– A touch of spicy cayenne can add a lot of heat to a dish without radically changing the flavor It is a mixture of ground chili peppers and can be used in a wide variety of cuisines.

CELERY SEED– The wild celery plant these seeds are from are on more and more menus emphasizing regional and local cuisine. The seeds add their pungent flavor to anything from cocktails to coleslaw and can be used whole or ground.

CHIVES– Leaves are used in many ways. May be used in salads, cream cheese, sandwiches, omelets, soups, and fish dishes.

CILANTRO– This herb is truly a love it or hate it proposition. Stems are quite sweet and can be added raw along with the leaves while the roots are prized by Thai chefs for curry pastes.

CINNAMON– Cinnamon adds sweetness and heat to sweet and savory dishes alike. Cinnamon sticks are often added whole to coffee, stews, rice, curries, or tangines and removed before serving. It is a staple in baked goods—a sprinkle makes even a simple bowl of oatmeal smell and taste great.

CLOVE– Often paired with cinnamon and nutmeg, cloves are dried flower buds that are sold both ground and whole. They have a warm, sweet flavor that works great with sweet and savory, like clove studded ham. For a more potent flavor grind them yourself.

CUMIN– Can be experienced in all kinds of dishes from Mexico, India and the Middle East. The toasted seeds can be used whole in dishes and eaten as is, or be ground right before use. Pre-ground cumin loses potency quickly, but can be helped by toasting first in a dry skillet over medium-low heat.

Herbs & Spices

DILL– The feathery leaves of the dill plant add light anise flavor to seafood, soups, salads, and lots of other dishes. Dill is almost always added at the very last minute. Keep fresh in the refrigerator by storing it in a glass of water with a plastic bag placed over the top.

GINGER– There are many ways to use this peppery root from fresh to dried and ground to pickled or crystallized. Each of these preparations adds unique flavors and textures to everything from stir-fries to roasted meats to classic ginger snaps.

MINT– Commonly associated with sweet treats, mint lends its cooling, peppery bite to plenty of savory dishes, particularly from the Middle East and North Africa. Perfect for summer-fresh salads or to liven up a sauce, leftover fresh mint can also be used to brew a fragrant tea which is equally tasty served hot or cold.

MUSTARD– Mustard is great to have around to add heat and a piquant flavor in sauces, dressings, marinades, and entrees. Whole mustard seeds are often part of the pickling spices, but are also a key part of many Indian curries where they are toasted in oil first until they pop.

NUTMEG– An aromatic spice with a sweet and spicy flavor. Nutmeg adds warmth and depth to foods but doesn't overpower other ingredients.

OREGANO– A pungent herb primarily found in Mediterranean and Mexican cuisines, it is one of the few herbs that survives the drying process relatively unscathed. Use dried oregano for longer stewing or dry rubs, but make sure to use half as much dry as you would fresh since the flavor is so intense. Oregano can also be used as a substitute for its close cousin marjoram.

PAPRIKA– Paprika has too often been relegated to the role of garnish, mostly because of its beautiful rich color. There are all sorts of paprika that can add flavors from mild to hot.

PARSLEY– Formerly regulated to the role of garnish, fresh parsley is coming into its own for its fresh flavor and great health benefits, but dried parsley lacks both flavor and color.

PEPPERCORN– Along with salt, black pepper is half of a team that is so fundamental to cooking that they get called upon nearly every time you need to spice up a dish. There are all sorts of peppercorns that each offer their own flavors and degrees of heat.

RED PEPPER– Dried red chili pepper sold either ground or in flakes, red pepper works well either added early to dishes that are going to cook for a while or simply shaken on near the very end. Because they vary greatly in terms of heat, taste your red pepper to see just how hot it is.

ROSEMARY– Can be used fresh or dried for long cooking in soups, meats, stews and more. Use sparingly at first and more if needed.

Herbs & Spices

SAGE– Used fresh. May be used in poultry and meat stuffings; in sausage and practically all meat combinations; in cheese and vegetable combinations, or curry.

TARRAGON– Experimenting with this anise-like herb in classic French favorites such as bearnaise sauce, creamy tarragon chicken, or fresh vinaigrette can help you learn how to use tarragon to lift flavors without overpowering a dish.

THYME– One of the most popular herbs in American and European cooking, thyme can be paired with nearly any kind of meat, poultry, fish, or vegetable. To use fresh thyme, peel off as many of the leaves as you can from the woody stem by running your fingers along the stem.

VANILLA– An aromatic spice with a warm flavor, vanilla is the seed pod of an orchid. It's available dried or as an extract.

HERB AND SPICE TIPS

In contrast to herbs, spices are nearly always dried and are mostly ground before using. Pre-ground spices lose their potency quickly, so they should be stored in airtight containers in a cool, dark place and be replaced around every six months. Whole spices retain their flavor longer (for up to five years) and can be used as is or quickly ground with mortar and pestle or an inexpensive coffee grinder (reserve one for spices to avoid coffee flavor).

To get the best flavor from your spices, "toast" them in a dry skillet over low heat, stirring frequently, until they start to release their aromas. Even ground spices can perk up a bit after a quick toast in a skillet, but ones that are too old and faded are generally beyond repair.

FRESH SEASONINGS

- In recipes, cut salt in half and add more fresh herbs and spices.
- When doubling a recipe, herbs and spices should only be increased by one and a half times. Taste, and then add some if necessary.
- Add sage, bay leaf and garlic at the beginning of the cooking process as they have a strong flavor. Herbs with more subtle aroma such as basil, parsley, fennel are best when added at the end of the cooking process to preserve their flavor.
- Delicate aromas can be lost due to overcooking.
- Cut or chop fresh herbs to expose more surface area. This will release more flavor.
- Here's a chart to convert dried herbs to fresh

1 tsp. dried herbs	=	1 Tbsp. fresh herbs
1/8 tsp. garlic powder	=	1 medium clove of garlic
1 tsp. onion powder	=	1 medium onion, finely chopped
1 tsp. ground ginger	=	1 tsp. grated fresh ginger

Cooking Vegetables

- Times on chart are for fresh, one pound vegetables.
- The cooking times are in minutes.
- NR = Not recommended.
- Steaming times begin when the water boils and creates steam.
- Vegetables are done when they are tender, but still crisp. (They should not be mushy.)

VEGETABLES	STEAM	MICRO.	BLANCH	BOIL	OTHER
Artichoke, whole	30-60	4-5 each	NR	25-40	NR
Artichoke, hearts	10-15	6-7	8-12	10-15	Stir-fry 10
Asparagus	8-10	4-6	2-3	5-12	Stir-fry pieces 5
Beans, green	5-15	6-12	4-5	10-20	Stir-fry 3-4
Beans, lima	10-20	8-12	5-10	20-30	NR
Beets	40-60	14-18	NR	30-60	Bake 60
Broccoli, spears	8-15	6-7	3-4	5-10	Blanch; Bake
Broccoli flowerets	5-6	4-5	2-3	4-5	Stir-fry 3-4
Brussels sprouts	6-12	7-8	4-5	5-10	Halve; Stir-fry 3-4
Cabbage, wedges	6-9	10-12	NR	10-15	
Carrots, whole	10-15	8-10	4-5	15-20	Bake 30-40
Carrots, sliced	4-5	4-7	3-4	5-10	Stir-fry 3-4
Cauliflower, whole	15-20	6-7	4-5	10-15	Blanch; Bake 20
Cauliflower, flowerets	6-10	3-5	3-4	5-8	Stir-fry 3-4
Corn, on cob	6-10	3-4	3-4	4-7	Soak 10; bake 375°
Corn, cut	4-6	2 per cup	2 12-4	3-4	Stir-fry 3-4
Eggplant, whole	15-30	7-10	10-15	10-15	Bake 30 at 400°
Eggplant, diced	5-6	5-6	3-4	5-10	Bake 10-15 425°
Greens, Collard, turnip	NR	18-20	8-15	30-60	Stir-fry 4-6
Greens, kale/beet	4-6	8-10	4-5	5-8	Stir-fry 2-3
Mushrooms	4-5	3-4	NR	3-4 /broth	Stir-fry or broil 4-5
Onions, whole	20-25	6-10	NR	20-30	Bake 60 at 325°
Onions, pearl	15-20	5-7	2-3	10-20	Braise 15-25
Parsnips	8-10	4-6	3-4	5-10	Bake 30 at 325°
Peas	3-5	5-7	1-2	8-12	Stir-fry 2-3
Peppers, bell	2-4	2-4	2-3	4-5	Stir-fry 2-3
Potatoes, whole	12-30	6-8	NR	20-30	Bake 40-60 at 400°
Potatoes, cut	10-12	8-10	NR	15-20	Bake 25-30 at 400°
Spinach	5-6	3-4	2-3	2-5	Stir-fry 2-3
Squash, sliced	5-10	3-6	2-3	5-10	NR
Squash, halves	15-40	6-10	NR	5-10	Bake 40-60 at 375°
Tomatoes	2-3	3-4	1-2	NR	Bake halves 8-15
Turnips, cubed	12-15	6-8	2-3	5-8	Stir-fry 2-3
Zucchini	5-10	3-6	2-3	5-10	Broil halves 5

Counting Calories

CANDIES, SNACKS & NUTS

Almonds	12 to 15	93
Cashews	6 to 8	88
Chocolate Bar (nut)	2 ounce bar	340
Coconut (shredded)	1 cup	344
English Toffee	1 piece	25
Fudge	1 ounce	115
Mints	5 very small	50
Peanuts (salted)	1 ounce	190
Peanuts (roasted)	1 cup	800
Pecans	6	104
Popcorn (plain)	1 cup	54
Potato Chips	10 medium chips	115
Pretzels	10 small sticks	35
Walnuts	8 to 10	100

DAIRY PRODUCTS

American Cheese	1 cube 1^1/$_8$ inch	100
Butter, margarine	1 level Tbsp.	100
Cheese (blue, cheddar, cream, Swiss)	1 ounce	105
Cottage Cheese (uncreamed)	1 ounce	25
Cream(light)	1 Tbsp.	30
Egg White	1	15
Egg Yolk	1	61
Eggs (boiled or poached)	2	160
Eggs (scrambled)	2	220
Eggs (fried)	1 medium	110
Yogurt (flavored)	4 ounces	60

DESSERTS

Cakes:

Angel Food Cake	2" piece	110
Cheesecake	2" piece	200
Chocolate Cake (iced)	2" piece	445
Fruit Cake	2" piece	115
Pound Cake	1 ounce piece	140
Sponge Cake	2" piece	120
Shortcake (with fruit)	1 avg. slice	300
Cupcake (iced)	1	185
Cupcake (plain)	1	145

Pudding:

Bread Pudding	^{1}/$_2$ cup	150
Flavored Pudding	^{1}/$_2$ cup	140

Pies:

Apple	1 piece	331
Blueberry	1 piece	290
Cherry	1 piece	355
Custard	1 piece	280

Counting Calories

Lemon Meringue	1 piece	305
Peach	1 piece	280
Pumpkin	1 piece	265
Rhubarb	1 piece	265
Ice Cream:		
Chocolate Ice Cream	½ cup	200
Vanilla Ice Cream	½ cup	150
Miscellaneous:		
Chocolate Eclair (custard)	1 small	250
Cookies (assorted)	1, 3-inch dia.	120
Cream Puff	1	296
Jello, all flavors	½ cup	78

BREADS & FLOUR FOODS

Baking Powder Biscuits	1 large or 2 small	129
Bran Muffin	1 medium	106
Corn Bread	1 small square	130
Dumpling	1 medium	70
Enriched White Bread	1 slice	60
French Bread	1 small slice	54
French Toast	1 slice	135
Macaroni and Cheese	1 cup	475
Melba Toast	1 slice	25
Noodles (cooked)	1 cup	200
Pancakes, wheat	1, 4-inch	60
Raisin Bread	1 slice	80
Rye Bread	1 slice	71
Saltines	1	17
Soda Crackers	1	23
Waffles	1	216
Whole Wheat Bread	1 slice	55

BREAKFAST CEREALS

Corn Flakes	1 cup	96
Cream of Wheat	1 cup	120
Oatmeal	1 cup	148
Rice Flakes	1 cup	105
Shredded Wheat	1 biscuit	100
Sugar Krisps	¾ cup	110

FISH & FOWL

Bass	4 ounces	105
Brook Trout	4 ounces	130
Crabmeat (canned)	3 ounces	85
Fish Sticks	5 sticks or 4 ounces	200
Haddock (canned)	1 fillet	158
Haddock (broiled)	4 ounces (steak)	207

Counting Calories

FRUITS

Apple (raw)	1 small	70
Banana	1 medium	85
Blueberries (frozen/unsweetened)	½ cup	45
Cantaloupe Melon	½ melon large	60
Cherries, fresh/whole	½ cup	40
Cranberries (sauce)	1 cup	54
Grapes	1 cup	65
Dates	3 or 4	95
Grapefruit (unsweetened)	½	55
Orange	1 medium	70
Peach (fresh)	1	35
Plums	2	50
Tangerine (fresh)	1	40
Watermelon	1" slice	60

MEATS

Bacon (crisp)	2 slices	95
Frankfurter	1	155
Hamburger (avg. fat/broiled)	3 ounces	245
Hamburger (lean/broiled)	3 ounces	185
Ham (broiled/lean)	3 ounces	200
Ham (baked)	1 slice	100
Lamb Leg Roast	3 ounces	235
Lamb Chop (rib)	3 ounces	300
Liver (fried)	3 ½ ounces	210
Meat Loaf	1 slice	100
Pork Chop (medium)	3 ounces	340
Pork Sausage	3 ounces	405
Roasts (beef)		
Loin Roast	3 ½ ounces	340
Pot Roast (round)	3 ½ ounces	200
Rib Roast	3 ½ ounces	260
Rump Roast	3 ½ ounces	340
Spareribs	1 piece, 3 ribs	123
Swiss Steak	3 ½ ounces	300
Veal Chop (medium)	3 ounces	185
Veal Roast	3 ounces	230

SALADS & DRESSINGS

Chef Salad/mayonnaise	1 Tbsp.	125
Chef Salad/French, Roquefort	1 Tbsp.	105
Cole Slaw (no dressing)	½ cup	102
Fruit Gelatin	1 square	139
Potato Salad (no dressing)	½ cup	184
French Dressing	1 Tbsp.	60
Mayonnaise	1 Tbsp.	110

Napkin Folding

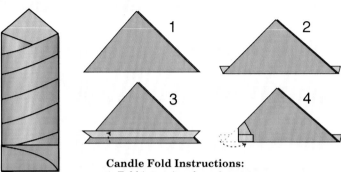

CANDLE

Candle Fold Instructions:
1. Fold into triangle, point at top.
2. Turn lower edge up about 1".
3. Turn over, folded edge down.
4. Roll tightly from left to right.
5. Tuck in corner. Stand upright.

DIAGONAL STRIPE

Diagonal Stripe Fold Instructions:
1. Fold edge A to edge B.
2. Fold edge A to edge B. Loose edges at top.
3. Roll down the top flap.
4. Roll down the second flap
5. Roll down the third flap
6. Fold sides back as pictured.

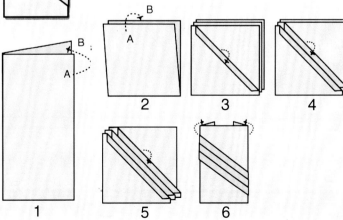

Table Settings

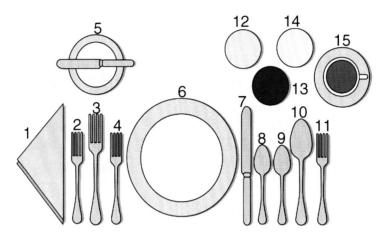

FORMAL TABLE SETTING

1. Napkin
2. Salad fork
3. Dinner fork
4. Dessert fork
5. Bread-and-butter plate, with spreader
6. Dinner plate
7. Dinner knife
8. Teaspoon
9. Teaspoon
10. Soup spoon
11. Cocktail fork
12. Water glass
13. Red-wine glass
14. White-wine glass
15. Coffee cup and saucer

GENERAL TABLE SETTING

1. Napkin
2. Salad fork
3. Dinner fork
4. Bread-and-butter plate
5. Salad plate
6. Dinner plate
7. Dinner knife
8. Teaspoon
9. Soup spoon
10. Water glass
11. Wine glass

- Don't put out utensils that won't ever be used.

- Bring the coffee cup and saucer to the table with the dessert.